JAMES MARTIN

Potato

**BAKED, MASHED, ROAST, FRIED –
OVER 100 RECIPES CELEBRATING POTATOES**

PHOTOGRAPHY BY JOHN CAREY

Hardie Grant

QUADRILLE

CONTENTS

INTRODUCTION

The world's most popular vegetable is used by cooks around the globe, from high-end restaurants to simple fire pits. The versatility of the humble potato is vast, as is the number of recipes in which it can be used. There are over 5,000 types of potato, each with a specific texture, taste and use. Each is not only unique in flavour but in where and how it is grown. It wasn't until the 16th century that potatoes were introduced to Europe from South America, but they have quickly become a staple food, as they are in many other parts of the world today. Some of the greatest potatoes I have ever tasted come from Peru and Chile, where many wild varieties can be found. It's amazing that the potato is now one of the most-produced crops in the world, alongside maize, wheat and rice.

Once used as currency, many people take the unassuming potato for granted, but it can be as highly prized as any of the finest ingredients. Some varieties are so seasonal that they are available for just a few weeks of the year, like Jersey Royals, which can only be produced on a small island and are so special because of the combination of climate, soil and the type of potato. While others, such as the Marabel, which is one of my favourite baking potatoes, with a crispy skin on the outside and a creamy texture on the inside that almost tastes like butter, can be harvested and stored for up to a year.

This cookbook explores different types of potato, from what makes a simple King Edward the best for roasting and an Estima not good for frying. I'll share what makes a great baking potato to the top choice for your fish and chips. Not only that, but I've combined over 100 recipes and techniques to guide you through a range of dishes from a pommes soufflé served in the finest of restaurants to the perfect humble mashed potato. There's everything from Tex-Mex BBQ filled potato skins to Japanese-inspired recipes where potatoes are baked in seaweed.

Potatoes have been a constant presence in my cooking life, from the first time I stepped foot in catering college making classic game chips – the accompaniment of choice for roast chicken and game birds – to working in three-star Michelin restaurants cooking Pommes Anna, used in every form of cookery and a staple in many a classic French cookbook from *Larousse Gastronomique* to *Le Répertoire de La Cuisine*. More recently, I have been involved in the running of SpudULike, the famous brand from the 1970s and 80s, which used to have queues round the block for their simple, but tasty, baked and filled potatoes. It's been great fun, not reinventing the brand but bringing it into the 21st century with a different twist, still keeping the classic taste at its core.

This book is a progression from my last book, *Butter*, as both ingredients, probably more so with potatoes, can be found across the globe. Their ability to grow in all manner of different climates is reflected in their use in an eclectic and international mix of recipes. Many of my mates who have Indian origins produce and cook some of my favourite food using humble ingredients like the potato, with the addition of a few spices, and whole dishes with wonderful flavours can be created for very little cost. Then you venture into the world of some of my other friends, like Clare Smyth and Sat Bains, both two- and three-star Michelin chefs, and see their trademark dishes using a simple single potato as the canvas for their food painting. In fact, Sat Bains's baked potato cooked in kombu and then in hot coals, opened up and topped with crème fraîche, butter and a dollop of caviar, creates two of the best-tasting mouthfuls of food you could wish for.

Fish and chips are still the nation's favourite, and rightly so. However, you wouldn't believe how technical the process can be to get the best fried chip, and I don't mean all that triple-cooked palaver. I'm talking about the extent some of the best fish and chip shops go to, to produce the great chip as we know it: it is a moving feast season by season, almost month by month, as they struggle to find the perfect potato with the right starch and sugar content to keep the standard the same. Everybody seems to think that they use the same potato all year round but that couldn't be further from the truth.

The potato is probably the one ingredient that was the catalyst for me becoming a chef. I always remember my grandfather used to cook simple, boiled new potatoes with butter, and serve them with poached haddock in milk. The main reason these were so good is because he was a brilliant gardener, not only of roses, but of potatoes, both of which need a great soil and manure to grow. I remember each season we used to 'earth up' or 'hill up', as he called it, and create 10–15-foot mounds of earth, which had to be perfectly drawn with a string line, and put in the potatoes every 40 inches using an old measuring stick cut to size. But it all paid dividends only a few months later when the crop decided to grow, as there is nothing that tastes as good as vegetables grown, dug and cooked the very same day.

Potatoes are the ultimate field-to-fork ingredient, so enjoy and experiment with this collection of recipes celebrating this often overlooked kitchen staple. While you are reading this book, I am probably either cooking potatoes in my restaurant kitchen or planting potatoes in my garden. For me, they are the number one most-used vegetable, but what makes them fascinating is the different varieties and types of cooking methods they are good for. This book hopes to explore just a small percentage of what is a vast subject regarding one of the most popular ingredients in the world... Enjoy it!

SNACKS, SOUPS & STARTERS

FOCACCIA WITH POTATOES AND ROSEMARY

\

SERVES 8

500g strong bread flour
7g sachet fast-action yeast
1 tablespoon salt
100ml olive oil, plus extra for greasing
350–400ml lukewarm water
400g new potatoes, cooked and sliced
a few sprigs of rosemary, chopped
extra virgin olive oil, for dipping

This bread dough not only looks and tastes fantastic, but it is easy to make, too. The most important thing to remember is that you must make the dough quite wet and sticky and knead it for a decent amount of time – I usually do it for ten minutes. Once out of the oven, you can brush the focaccia with even more olive oil. Use extra virgin olive oil to dip it into, as this has a better flavour.

In a stand mixer, mix the flour, yeast and salt with half the oil and lukewarm water. Using the dough hook, knead the dough for 5–10 minutes – it should be sticky.

Oil a shallow rectangular baking tray. Drop the dough in and stretch out to the corners. Leave to prove for 1 hour.

Preheat the oven to 220°C (200°C fan)/425°F/gas 7.

Dot the dough with the potatoes and rosemary and drizzle over the remaining oil. Bake for 20 minutes until the dough and potatoes are golden. Serve with extra virgin olive oil for dipping.

10-DAY FERMENTED POTATO BREAD

\

SERVES 6

FOR THE FERMENTED POTATOES
500g potatoes, peeled, cooked and
    riced
20g salt

FOR THE BREAD DOUGH
500g fermented potatoes
300g thick full-fat yogurt
600g plain flour, plus extra for dusting
5g fast-action yeast
15g salt

FOR THE CORIANDER SALSA
1 small bunch of coriander, chopped
1 red onion, diced
400g mixed Isle of Wight tomatoes,
    diced
2 tablespoons sherry vinegar
2 tablespoons olive oil
sea salt and freshly ground black
    pepper

This was an idea we had in the restaurant and is a great recipe that came off the back of me messing around with soda bread, but it uses fermented potatoes, which alter the taste dramatically. I've served it with a salsa, but it is also great with hummus or a simple roasted red pepper dip.

To make the fermented potatoes, place the potatoes and salt in a ziplock bag, squeeze out all the air, seal, then pop in the fridge for 10 days.

To make the dough, place all the ingredients in a stand mixer fitted with the dough hook and knead for 5 minutes. Pop into a bowl, cover with clingfilm, then chill in the fridge for 24 hours.

Preheat the oven to 220°C (200°C fan)/425°F/gas 7.

Dust a work surface with flour. Roll out the dough into 6 large oblong shapes (roughly 8 x 15cm), pop onto a floured baking tray and bake for 15 minutes until crisp and golden.

To make the coriander salsa, mix all the ingredients together in a bowl and season to taste.

Serve the potato bread with the coriander salsa.

BERKSWELL CHEESE GNOCCHI WITH ROASTED BUTTERNUT SOUP
\
SERVES 4

FOR THE GNOCCHI

200g potatoes, peeled, cooked and riced

4 egg yolks

60g Italian '00' flour, plus extra for dusting

30g Berkswell cheese, finely grated

1 teaspoon salt

50ml olive oil

2 sprigs of rosemary, leaves picked and roughly chopped

FOR THE SOUP

2 tablespoons olive oil

1 onion, finely diced

1 butternut squash (about 1kg), peeled, deseeded and cut into 1cm dice

2 garlic cloves, finely chopped

500ml chicken stock

sea salt and freshly ground black pepper

TO SERVE

2 tablespoons coriander cress

2 tablespoons olive oil

Gnocchi is one of the true joys to make in a kitchen, using dry, cooked and riced potatoes with the addition of egg yolks and flour. You can add various cheeses, the classic being Parmesan, but Berkswell or a blue cheese works fantastically with this soup. If you want to make gnocchi in advance, the best way is to blanch them first, then freeze them and use as required. This soup works equally well with cauliflower instead of the butternut squash.

To make the gnocchi, mix the potato, egg yolks, '00' flour, cheese and salt together in a bowl until it just forms a soft dough. Check the seasoning.

Divide the mixture in half and then, on a floured surface, roll each piece into a long sausage shape, about 1.25cm in diameter. With a sharp knife, cut each sausage into 2.5cm pieces of gnocchi.

Bring a large saucepan of salted water to the boil. Drop the gnocchi into the water and cook for 1–2 minutes, or until they float. Remove from the water with a slotted spoon and place onto a plate lined with kitchen paper.

Heat a frying pan until hot, add the oil, rosemary and the gnocchi and fry for 1–2 minutes until golden brown and just crispy. Drain onto kitchen paper.

To make the soup, heat a frying pan until hot, then add the oil, onion and squash and fry for 1–2 minutes.

Add the garlic and cook for 1 minute, then add the stock and bring to the boil. Simmer for about 5–6 minutes until the squash is tender.

Pour in batches into a food processor and blitz to a fine purée.

Place the soup in a clean saucepan and season with salt and black pepper. Return to the heat to warm through.

To serve, ladle the soup into soup plates. Pile some gnocchi in the centre of each plate, then scatter over the coriander cress and drizzle with the olive oil.

POTATO, ONION AND BACON SODA BREAD WITH HOMEMADE BUTTER

\
SERVES 4

FOR THE SODA BREAD
170g wholemeal self-raising flour
170g plain flour, plus extra for dusting
½ teaspoon salt
1 teaspoon bicarbonate of soda
300ml buttermilk
200g potatoes, peeled, cooked and
    diced
4 spring onions, diced
125g bacon lardons, fried

FOR THE HOMEMADE BUTTER
750ml double cream
sea salt

We all know about my love of butter from my previous book, so I had to include a homemade version to enjoy alongside this bread. This is one of the dishes that we make at the restaurant for staff food, as it's super tasty and so simple to prepare.

Preheat the oven to 200°C (180°C fan)/400°F/gas 6.

Put all the soda bread ingredients in a large bowl and mix to form a dough. Shape into 2 circles and push down – they should be 15cm in diameter and 3cm deep. Place on a baking tray dusted with flour, dust the bread with a little more flour and cut a cross onto the top. Bake for 15–20 minutes.

To make the butter, put the double cream into a stand mixer fitted with the whisk attachment and beat until it separates. Take the solid part and put it in a clean tea towel. Form into a tight parcel and squeeze out the liquid. Place onto greaseproof paper and add sea salt to taste, then shape it into a sausage using the greaseproof paper.

Serve slices of the soda bread spread with the homemade butter.

ARBROATH SMOKIE SCOTCH EGGS WITH CURRY MAYO

\

MAKES 6

FOR THE SCOTCH EGGS

8 Arbroath smokies, skinned and
    flaked
1kg potatoes, peeled, cooked and
    mashed
6 soft-boiled eggs
75g plain flour, seasoned
2 eggs, beaten
175g panko breadcrumbs
vegetable oil, for deep-frying

FOR THE CURRY MAYO

3 egg yolks
1 tablespoon Dijon mustard
1 tablespoon white wine vinegar
200ml vegetable oil
1 tablespoon curry powder
sea salt and freshly ground black
    pepper

Traditionally made with sausage meat, these Scotch-eggs-cum-fishcakes make an amazing meal. They are also a lot easier to cook than Scotch eggs as the filling is already cooked, but the process of making them is still the same. Make sure the eggs are soft-boiled, which usually takes about 6 minutes, and carefully envelop the egg in the coating. I serve these with a curry mayonnaise as I think the taste works so well with the Arbroath smokies.

To make the curry mayo, whisk together the egg yolks, mustard and vinegar in a bowl. Slowly drizzle in the oil, whisking continuously until thickened.

Mix the curry powder with 15ml water to make a paste, then add to the mayo. Season and whisk to combine. Set aside.

For the Scotch eggs, mix the fish with the potato, season and divide into 6 even-sized portions. Flatten each into a rough circle. Place an egg on top and wrap the mixture around the eggs, encompassing them completely.

Place the flour in one bowl, the beaten eggs in a second and the breadcrumbs in a third. Dip each Scotch egg in flour, then beaten egg, then flour and egg again, and then dip into the breadcrumbs. Gently reshape into rounds.

Heat the vegetable oil in a deep-fat fryer or large pan to 160°C (325°F) and deep-fry the Scotch eggs for 3–4 minutes until golden and crispy. Drain onto kitchen paper.

Serve with a big dollop of curry mayo.

IRISH FISH SOUP

\

SERVES 6

400g clams
25g butter
1 shallot, finely diced
25g plain flour
400ml full-fat milk
100ml double cream
400g potatoes, peeled, diced and
    cooked
1 small bunch of chives, chopped
200g sweetcorn
200g white crab meat
100g brown crab meat

TO SERVE
double cream, to drizzle (optional)
olive oil, to drizzle (optional)
warm crusty bread

I had this soup while on a visit to Northern Ireland and loved it so much I always wanted to put it in a book. It's kind of like a chowder, but it uses amazing clams and brown and white crab meat to add depth of flavour.

Heat a large pan with a lid, add 100ml water and the clams, then pop the lid on and cook for 3 minutes. Drain, saving the liquor, then pick the meat from the shells and put to one side.

In the same pan, melt the butter, then add the shallot and cook for a minute or two until softened. Stir in the flour, mix thoroughly, then add the clam liquor, milk and cream, stirring continuously. Simmer gently for 5 minutes.

Add the potatoes and cook with the lid on for a further 2–3 minutes.

Season well and add the chives, sweetcorn, crab and cooked clams. Gently warm through.

To serve, ladle into bowls, drizzle with extra cream and olive oil, if desired, and serve with crusty bread.

CRISP SANDWICH

\
MAKES 1

vegetable oil, for deep-frying
1 large Chippies Choice potato, peeled
50g butter, softened
2 thick-cut slices of white bread
sea salt
malt vinegar

Why not?! The question is: to butter or not to butter...? You know it makes sense!

Heat the vegetable oil in a deep-fat fryer or large pan to 170°C (340°F).

Thinly slice the potato on a mandoline. Deep-fry until crisp, then drain onto kitchen paper.

Spread the butter over both slices of the bread. Pile up the crisps on one slice, sprinkle over some salt and vinegar and sit the other slice on top. Cut in half to serve.

COQUILLES ST JACQUES
\
SERVES 6

50g butter
50g plain flour
500ml full-fat milk
1 small bunch of parsley, chopped
12 scallops
300g prawns

FOR THE TOPPING
600g potatoes, peeled and diced
50g butter
2 egg yolks

I used to take the mick out of French chefs saying this is their fancy fish pie, but it does taste bloody amazing! And just look at it... super indulgent, yes, but a classic that should never be forgotten.

Preheat the oven to 200°C (180°C fan)/400°F/gas 6.

To make the white sauce, melt the butter in a pan, then whisk in the flour and cook out for 2 minutes. Add the milk and whisk to combine, then simmer until bubbling. Stir in the parsley.

Put the scallops and prawns into scallop shells and pour over the sauce. Set aside to cool.

Cook the potatoes in boiling salted water for 20 minutes until soft, drain and then pass through a ricer into a bowl. Mix with the butter and egg yolks.

Pipe the potato mixture around the edges of the scallop shells then sit on a baking tray and bake for 15–20 minutes.

CROQUETTES WITH POTATOES, HAM AND MANCHEGO

SERVES 4

100g butter
225g plain flour
1 teaspoon sweet paprika
550ml full-fat milk
4 eggs
100g Manchego, cubed
200g potatoes, peeled, cooked and
    diced
6 slices of Iberico ham, sliced
2 teaspoons chopped flat-leaf parsley
2 eggs, beaten
100g panko breadcrumbs
vegetable oil, for deep-frying
sea salt and freshly ground black
    pepper

TO SERVE
lemon mayo (page 58)
grated Manchego

This recipe is based on the famous Spanish croquettes you will find in nearly every tapas restaurant. The filling is similar to a very thick béchamel or white sauce, with the addition of cooked ingredients, which is then cooled. Once cold, it's best to use wet hands to prevent the mixture sticking to them when rolling it into croquettes or balls, before coating the croquettes in flour, egg and breadcrumbs and deep-frying them.

Put the butter into a pan over a medium heat. When it is foaming, add 150g of the flour and the sweet paprika, then whisk in the milk. Cook gently over a very low heat for 3 minutes, stirring constantly.

Remove the mixture from the heat and leave it to cool for a few minutes, then beat in the eggs, cheese, potatoes, ham, parsley, ½ teaspoon of salt and some black pepper to taste.

Chill the mixture in the fridge for 2 hours, then divide and shape into 8 x 2cm sausages.

Place the remaining flour in one bowl, the beaten eggs in a second and the breadcrumbs in a third. Dip each croquette in the flour, then egg, then breadcrumbs.

Heat the oil in a deep-fat fryer or large pan to 180°C (350°F). Drop the croquettes into the hot oil and cook in batches for 1–2 minutes until crisp and golden.

Drain onto kitchen paper and serve immediately with lemon mayo and grated Manchego.

SALT COD CROQUETTES WITH ROASTED RED PEPPER SAUCE

\

SERVES 6

FOR THE CROQUETTES

300g salt cod, soaked overnight in cold
   water
300g mashed potato
100g plain flour, seasoned
2 eggs, beaten
100g fresh breadcrumbs
vegetable oil, for deep-frying

FOR THE SAUCE

1 large jar of roasted red peppers,
   chopped
2 garlic cloves, chopped
1 small bunch of oregano, leaves picked
1 onion, sliced
50ml olive oil

Salt cod or bacalao must be soaked in cold water overnight, before cooking in either milk or water. None of the flavour is lost – if anything, it's intensified. Some of the best salt cod I have tasted is from Thule Ventus, in Shetland. You can buy it online and when you do, try salt piltock, which is amazing but is made with coley. Up north they call these hairy tatties! And they are usually made like a fishcake.

Drain the salt cod, then put in a pan, cover with water and poach for 15 minutes. Drain.

Flake the fish in a bowl, add the potato and roll into 8 x 3cm sausages. You should have about 12 croquettes.

Place the flour in one bowl, the beaten eggs in a second and the breadcrumbs in a third. Dip each croquette in the flour, then eggs, then breadcrumbs.

Heat the oil in a deep-fat fryer or large pan to 170°C (340°F). Drop the croquettes into the hot oil and cook in batches for 1–2 minutes until crisp and golden.

Meanwhile, put all the sauce ingredients into a pan and warm through for 5 minutes.

To serve, spoon the sauce onto a platter and top with the deep-fried croquettes.

HAM HOCK BROTH AND
SOFT-BOILED DEEP-FRIED EGGS

\

SERVES 6

1 ham hock
600ml ham stock from cooked hock
50ml white wine
50g butter
1 bunch of asparagus, peeled and
    sliced
50g fresh peas
1 small bunch of chives, chopped
300g cooked Jersey Royals
25g plain flour, seasoned
1 egg, beaten
75g panko breadcrumbs
6 soft-boiled eggs
vegetable oil, for deep-frying

TO DECORATE
wild garlic flowers (optional)

This is a great-tasting soup that uses up leftover cooked potatoes. I use Jersey Royals, because whenever this variety is in season, so are asparagus and new season fresh peas. You don't have to cook your own ham as you can easily make this with water or chicken stock and just add chopped cooked ham. It's an entire meal in a bowl.

Place the ham hock in a large pan and cover with water. Gently simmer for 2 hours. Remove the hock from the stock, retaining the stock. Remove the fat layer and discard, then shred the meat.

In a large pan, gently warm the wine and 600ml of the ham stock. Add three-quarters of the butter and, when melted, pop in the asparagus, shredded ham and peas. Cook gently for 2 minutes. Add the chives.

In a small frying pan, melt the remaining butter. Add the potatoes, crush and cook until they are warmed through.

Place the flour in one bowl, the beaten eggs in a second and the breadcrumbs in a third. Dip each soft-boiled egg in the flour, then eggs, then breadcrumbs.

Heat the oil in a deep-fat fryer or large pan to 170°C (340°F). Deep-fry the eggs for 1 minute, then drain onto kitchen paper.

To serve, spoon a mound of potatoes into the bowls, top with a halved egg, then spoon over the ham mixture and sprinkle with wild garlic flowers, if using.

WATERCRESS SOUP WITH JERSEY ROYALS

SERVES 6

750ml full-fat milk
100ml double cream
500g cooked Jersey Royals
2 bunches of watercress
1 small bunch of parsley
sea salt and freshly ground black
    pepper

TO SERVE
25ml olive oil
150ml double cream, softly whipped
a few sprigs of watercress

As you can see from the colour, this soup is so vibrant and fresh, which is why you add the watercress right at the very end to retain that colour. You don't have to use Jersey Royals, any potatoes will do. This soup also freezes very well, plus you can add prawns, smoked salmon and smoked haddock, which will turn it into a full-blown meal.

Heat a large pan, add the milk and cream and warm through. Add half the cooked potatoes. Bring to the boil, then simmer for 2–3 minutes. Add the watercress and parsley, then pour into a food processor and blitz until smooth. Season, then pour back into the pan and gently heat through.

Dice the remaining potatoes, spoon into bowls, then ladle in the soup and drizzle with olive oil and cream and dot with the watercress to serve.

EEL POTATO CAKES
WITH BEURRE BLANC

\

SERVES 4

FOR THE EEL POTATO CAKES

300g potatoes, peeled, cooked and
    riced
1 egg yolk
2 spring onions, sliced thinly
200g smoked eels, flaked
75g plain flour, seasoned
2 eggs, beaten
100g panko breadcrumbs
vegetable oil, for deep-frying sea salt
    and freshly ground black pepper

FOR THE BEURRE BLANC

100g bacon lardons
1 shallot, finely diced
50ml white wine
25ml double cream
300g cold butter, cubed
juice of ½ lemon
2 tablespoons chopped chives

Smoked eel is a true culinary delight and I urge you to try it, either in a salad with crème fraîche and crispy bacon or a fine-dining-style dish with pan-fried duck liver. I like to put it in a simple potato cake, served with a classic beurre blanc. The bacon cuts through the buttery sauce alongside a good squeeze of lemon juice.

To make the beurre blanc, add the bacon to a non-stick pan and fry until crisp. Add the shallot and cook for another minute, then splash in the wine and cream. When bubbling, take off the heat and whisk in the butter, lemon juice and chopped chives.

To make the potato cakes, gently mix together the potato, egg yolk, spring onions and eel and season. Roll into 10cm wide patties, about 3cm tall.

Place the flour in one bowl, the beaten eggs in a second and the breadcrumbs in a third. Dip each potato cake in the flour, then egg, then breadcrumbs. Gently reshape each one into a ball.

Heat the oil in a deep-fat fryer or large pan to 170°C (340°F). Fry the potato cakes in batches for 3–4 minutes, then drain onto kitchen paper.

To serve, spoon the beurre blanc into the centre of plates and top with the eel potato cakes.

FRIED CHICKEN AND POTATO SKINS WITH CHIPOTLE SAUCE

\

SERVES 6

vegetable oil, for deep-frying
1 tablespoon paprika
2 teaspoons onion salt
1 teaspoon freshly ground black
   pepper
½ teaspoon celery salt
½ teaspoon dried sage
½ teaspoon garlic powder
½ teaspoon ground allspice
1 teaspoon dried oregano
1 teaspoon dried marjoram
200g plain flour
2 eggs, beaten
600g chicken fillets
6 jacket potato skins, cut into 4

FOR THE CHIPOTLE SAUCE
2 garlic cloves, crushed
1 red pepper, cored and diced
100g brown sugar
1 teaspoon smoked paprika
1 teaspoon celery salt
1 teaspoon chipotle chilli flakes
1 tablespoon Worcestershire sauce
25ml black treacle
300ml tomato ketchup
1 teaspoon chipotle chilli paste

This came from one of my chefs as his TV dinner and it beats pizza any day! The key is the combination of spices, which all work well together. Served with a simple sauce that is just thrown into a pan and boiled for 2 minutes, it's quick, too.

Heat the oil in a deep-fat fryer or large pan to 170°C (340°F).

Mix all the spices and herbs with the flour in a bowl. Place the beaten egg in a bowl. Dip the chicken fillets in the egg, then the spicy flour mixture.

Deep-fry the chicken in batches for 2–3 minutes, then drain onto kitchen paper. Add the potato skins and fry for 3 minutes until crisp, then drain onto kitchen paper.

To make the sauce, put all the ingredients into a non-stick pan, bring to the boil, then simmer for 2 minutes.

To serve, put the potato skins in a large bowl, top with the chicken, then spoon over the sauce.

JERSEY ROYALS WITH ASPARAGUS, POACHED DUCK EGGS AND HOLLANDAISE

\

SERVES 4

500g Jersey Royals
4 duck eggs
1 teaspoon white wine vinegar
1 bunch of asparagus
200g broad beans, podded
200g white crab meat
sea salt and freshly ground black
    pepper

FOR THE HOLLANDAISE
2 egg yolks
1 teaspoon white wine vinegar
250g butter, melted
1 small bunch of chives, chopped, plus
    chive flowers to garnish (optional)

This is a less fiddly variant of a dish that we serve in the restaurant. I love podded broad beans because they bring back childhood memories of my granddad's veg plot, and the poached duck eggs are a true delight. The key to poaching these is to cook them for longer than conventional chicken eggs as they are slightly bigger. Once cooked, you can keep them in ice-cold water and reheat them in boiling water when needed.

Cook the potatoes in boiling salted water for 12 minutes until cooked. Drain and cool slightly.

To poach the duck eggs, bring a large pan of boiling water to the boil, add the vinegar and, using a whisk, make a whirlpool in the centre. Break an egg into the centre of the whirlpool and cook for 3–4 minutes. Using a slotted spoon, scoop the egg into a bowl of iced water and repeat with the remaining eggs.

Cut the asparagus spears into thirds, and blanch in boiling water for 2 minutes with the broad beans.

To make the hollandaise, whisk the egg yolks with the vinegar, then add the melted butter slowly, whisking continuously. Season and add the chives.

To serve, reheat the poached eggs in boiling water for 30 seconds and drain. Spoon the hollandaise sauce onto a platter and top with the potatoes, asparagus, beans and crab. Finish with the eggs, chives and chive flowers, if using.

NIBBLES WITH WARM CHEESE FONDUE

\

SERVES 6

FOR THE FONDUE
100ml white wine
3 teaspoons cornflour
500g Cheddar, grated
500g Gruyère, grated
100ml crème fraîche
sea salt and freshly ground black
    pepper

TO SERVE
24 baby potatoes (about 400g)
12 slices of pancetta, halved lengthways
400g chorizo chunks
18 baby carrots
2 small bags of radishes
1 jar of cornichons and pickled onions,
    drained
1 endive, leaves separated

This was simply the most popular dish in the book when this photograph was taken. The cooked potatoes wrapped in pancetta work brilliantly hot or cold and dunked in the fondue – what could be nicer? For vegetarians, just use good-quality potatoes and veg like fresh radishes, which taste amazing.

Preheat the oven to 200°C (180°C fan)/400°F/gas 6.

Cook the potatoes in boiling salted water for 12–15 minutes until just soft. Drain and leave to cool.

Wrap each potato in a slice of pancetta, pop onto a roasting tray and roast for 15 minutes.

Pop the chorizo into a small roasting tray and roast for 15 minutes alongside the potatoes.

To make the fondue, whisk all the ingredients together in a non-stick pan, gently whisking continuously until warmed through. Pour into a fondue dish and keep warm.

Serve with the carrots, radishes, chorizo, baby potatoes, cornichons and onions, and endive for dipping.

LEEK AND POTATO SOUP WITH CRISPY BACON AND BLUE CHEESE TOASTS

\

SERVES 4

FOR THE SOUP
2 leeks, sliced
300g potatoes, sliced
100ml double cream
500ml full-fat milk
sea salt and freshly ground black pepper

FOR THE TOASTS
300g stilton, crumbled, plus extra
   to serve
50ml double cream
4 slices of toasted sourdough

TO SERVE
4 slices of crispy bacon, crumbled
1 tablespoon double cream
1 tablespoon olive oil
crispy julienne leeks

By slicing the potatoes and leeks very thinly, I actually made this entire dish in less than 10 minutes. Any potatoes will do as they are used as a thickener once blended. You don't have to serve the soup with the toasts, you can just enjoy it as it is. If you are going to make the crispy leeks, fry them in oil over a medium heat because if they brown too much, they can become bitter and unpleasant.

Place the leeks, potatoes, cream and milk in a pan, bring to the boil, then simmer for 6–8 minutes. Transfer to a food processor and blitz until smooth. Season to taste.

Preheat the grill to high.

Mix the cheese and cream together, spread over the toast, place on a baking tray and grill until hot and bubbling.

Dvide between bowls and top with extra crumbled stilton and the bacon. Drizzle with the cream and oil, scatter over the crispy leeks and serve with the toasts alongside.

PISTOU SOUP

\

SERVES 6–8

FOR THE SOUP

4 tablespoons extra virgin olive oil
1 onion, chopped
1 garlic clove, chopped
1 leek, cut into small dice
1 medium carrot, cut into small dice
1 courgette, cut into small dice
2 medium potatoes, peeled and cut
    into small dice
75g French beans, topped and tailed
    and cut into 4 pieces
75g spaghetti
10 plum tomatoes, skinned, deseeded
    and diced
100g frozen peas
100g frozen broad beans, blanched
    and peeled
400g can haricot beans, washed and
    drained
sea salt and freshly ground black pepper

FOR THE PISTOU

60g basil leaves
1 garlic clove
1 tomato, skinned and deseeded
75g Parmesan, grated
100ml extra virgin olive oil

This dish does take a lot of chopping, as you can see from the ingredients list but it is definitely worth the effort. It's a classic soup that never fails, as it uses an amazing array of vegetables, but the most important thing is not to overcook them, as this will kill the taste. The pistou is a form of pesto that goes in and helps flavour the soup at the end.

To make the soup, heat a large pan over a medium heat and add the olive oil. Fry the onion, garlic, leek, carrot, courgette and potatoes, without colouring, for 4–5 minutes.

Next, add the French beans, top with water to cover slightly and bring to the boil.

Place the spaghetti in a clean tea towel and roll it up and over the edge of a worktop, pressing it backwards and forwards to break the pasta into small pieces, then add to the soup.

Add the diced tomatoes and simmer for 15 minutes to cook the pasta. With 4 minutes remaining, add the peas, broad and haricot beans and heat through.

While the soup is cooking, place the pistou ingredients in a food processor and blend to a pesto-like paste.

Remove the soup from the heat and stir in the pistou, season well and serve straight away.

CHEESY POTATO WAFFLES

\
SERVES 4

FOR THE WAFFLES
250g plain flour
1 teaspoon baking powder
1 teaspoon caster sugar
3 eggs
200ml full-fat milk
2 tablespoons chopped parsley
15g butter, melted

FOR THE FILLINGS
1 large potato, peeled, diced and
  blanched
3 cabbage leaves, blanched and diced
4 spring onions, sliced
4 slices of bacon, cooked and diced

TO FINISH
300g Cheddar, grated

The batter for these waffles is so easy to make and once you own a waffle machine there is no looking back, as you can add so many flavours and toppings to a classic batter. This recipe was also a popular one with my team – all that was left was the cheese on the tray... some say that's the best bit!

Preheat the grill to high. Heat a waffle machine to high, according to the manufacturer's instructions.

To make the waffles, whisk all the ingredients together, then fold through the fillings.

Ladle the mixture into a waffle machine and cook until golden. Then pop the waffles onto a baking tray, top with cheese and place under the hot grill until bubbling.

SAMOSAS

\
MAKES 24

FOR THE FILLING
1 tablespoon vegetable oil, plus extra
 for deep-frying
1 onion, diced
1 large potato, peeled and finely diced
3 garlic cloves, crushed
2 teaspoons garam masala
100ml vegetable stock
100g frozen peas
a few sprigs of coriander, chopped
sea salt and freshly ground black
 pepper

FOR THE PASTRY
300g plain flour, plus extra for dusting
15g salt
3 tablespoons vegetable oil

TO SERVE
mango chutney
mint and yogurt dip
lime wedges
a few coriander leaves

Any regular viewer of my show will know that Dipna and her dad Gulu taught me how to make, shape and cook samosas. Once you master the skill, which I have yet to perfect, they taste amazing. The fillings can be whatever you want, and you can also invest in one of those little samosa rolling pins, which can make your life either easier or more difficult, as when I see them roll the dough it spins at the same time... it's like magic!

Heat a large non-stick pan and add the oil, then fry the onion, potato, garlic and garam masala for 5 minutes. Add the vegetable stock and cook until the potatoes are just cooked, then stir through the peas and coriander. Season and set aside to cool.

To make the pastry, add all the ingredients to a stand mixer fitted with the dough hook. Mix together, adding enough water to bind the ingredients, then knead gently on a floured work surface for 5 minutes. Pop into a bowl, cover with clingfilm and chill the fridge for 30 minutes.

Dust a work surface with flour. Divide the dough into 12 even-sized balls, then roll each one into a 15cm circle and cut each circle in half.

Brush the edges of a dough half with a little water, then form into a cone shape in your hands. Fill with 1 tablespoon of the filling and press the top together to seal. Repeat to make the rest of the samosas.

Heat the oil in a deep-fat fryer or large pan to 180°C (350°F).

Deep-fry the samosas for 8 minutes, working in batches, and drain onto kitchen paper. Serve with mango chutney, mint and yogurt dip, lime wedges and a sprinkle of coriander.

POTATO AND CHEESE SCONES

\
MAKES 12

450g strong white flour, plus extra
   for dusting
2 teaspoons baking powder
pinch of salt
100g cold butter, diced
300ml full-fat milk
150g potatoes, peeled, cooked and
   diced
150g Cheddar, grated
1 small bunch of chives, chopped
1 egg
1 egg yolk, beaten, for egg wash

TO SERVE
butter
4 slices of crispy cooked pancetta,
   per serving

I love making scones, sweet or savoury, as the mixture is so easy to put together. As you can see from my method, wherever possible, make them by hand and use your fingertips to rub in the butter, which will help the end product. If you use a machine, you tend to overmix them, which causes the scones to shrink and their texture to be tougher.

Preheat the oven to 220°C (200°C fan)/425°F/gas 7.

Mix the flour, baking powder and salt in a bowl, add the butter and, using your fingertips, rub it in until the mixture resembles breadcrumbs. Add the milk, potatoes, cheese, chives and egg and mix until you have a smooth dough.

Roll out the dough on a lightly floured surface until 2cm thick. Cut out scones using a 7cm cutter, rerolling the scraps until you have 12 scones. Brush the tops with the egg wash.

Bake for 10–12 minutes. Remove from the oven and allow to cool slightly, then split and top with butter and pancetta.

POTATO CAKES WITH SMOKED SALMON AND CRÈME FRAÎCHE

\
SERVES 2

250g Maris Piper potatoes, peeled
  and diced
25g butter
75g plain flour
1 teaspoon baking powder
vegetable oil, for frying

TO SERVE
200g smoked salmon
75g crème fraîche
a few chives, chopped

This simple brunch dish is very quick to make, super tasty and can be served with salad or a little wilted spinach. Or enjoy it with some chopped green chilli like my team do.

Add the potatoes to a pan of salted water and bring to the boil. Cook for 12–15 minutes until the potatoes are cooked. Drain, then pop back in the pan and steam-dry.

Add the butter and mash the potatoes, then beat in the flour along with the baking powder. Shape into 2 discs about 15cm wide and 2cm deep.

Heat a non-stick pan over a medium heat. Add the oil and fry the potato cakes for 2–3 minutes on each side until golden.

To serve, pop the potato cakes onto plates and top with the smoked salmon, crème fraîche and chives.

POTATO, ROCKET AND TRUFFLE SALAD

\
SERVES 4

600g new potatoes
1 large bag of rocket
100g Parmesan, shaved

FOR THE DRESSING
100ml olive oil
50ml white wine vinegar
sea salt and freshly ground black
  pepper

TO SERVE
freshly grated truffle

It sounds very indulgent, but you don't have to use fresh truffle for this salad, adding a little truffle oil in the dressing will work too; however, treat truffle oil with caution, as it can overpower everything. The reason why I use olive oil, not extra virgin olive oil, is it that it doesn't compete for flavour. Adding crispy bacon or cooked shredded chicken works well too.

Cook the potatoes for 12–15 minutes in boiling salted water until tender. Drain.

Whisk all the ingredients for the dressing together with a splash of water in a large bowl and add the potatoes while still warm.

Spoon the potatoes onto a serving platter and scatter with the rocket, Parmesan and truffle. Season with freshly ground black pepper.

PATATAS BRAVAS

\
SERVES 4

1kg King Edward potatoes, peeled
   and cubed
100ml olive oil

FOR THE SAUCE
1 shallot, diced
25ml olive oil
3 garlic cloves, crushed
400g can chopped tomatoes
1 tablespoon pimentón
1 teaspoon chilli powder
1 teaspoon salt, plus extra to serve

I love Spanish food, and I love this type of dish where simplicity is key. The addition of pimentón, the smoked pepper powder that you buy either sweet or hot, is crucial here, as this recipe just doesn't work with anything else.

Preheat the oven to 220°C (200°C fan)/425°F/gas 7.

Place the potatoes into a roasting tray, drizzle in the olive oil, then toss and roast for 45 minutes until golden and crisp.

Meanwhile, to make the sauce, fry the shallot in the oil for 2–3 minutes until translucent. Add the remaining sauce ingredients and gently bubble for 15 minutes.

To serve, pop the potatoes into tapas dishes, sprinkle over the salt and top with the sauce.

APPLE AND POTATO RÖSTI WITH BLACK PUDDING
\
SERVES 2

25ml vegetable oil
4 slices of black pudding
2 eggs

FOR THE RÖSTI
1 large potato, peeled and grated
1 apple, grated
1 tablespoon crème fraîche
1 egg yolk
25g butter
15ml olive oil
sea salt and freshly ground black
  pepper

The combination of these flavours really does work, simple grated apple and potato together with crème fraîche and egg yolk stops the rösti from becoming too fatty. People always have their favourite black pudding, but mine is from Laverstoke Park Farm, which you can buy online.

Preheat the oven to 200°C (180°C fan)/400°F/gas 6.

Pour the oil into a frying pan, add the slices of black pudding and fry for 2 minutes on each side. Transfer to a baking tray and cook in the oven for 5 minutes.

Pop the potato and apple into a clean tea towel and squeeze out all the excess liquid. Transfer to a bowl and mix with the crème fraîche and egg yolk. Pop into a frying pan over a medium heat with the butter and oil and season. Fry for 4–5 minutes until golden, then flip over and repeat on the other side.

Meanwhile, heat a separate frying pan, add a drizzle of vegetable oil and fry the eggs until crisp.

To serve, cut the rösti in half, sit on plates and top each with 2 slices of black pudding and an egg, then season.

SMOKED SALMON WITH HOMEMADE SALAD CREAM

\

SERVES 2

300g smoked salmon
few chives, snipped
lemon wedges

FOR THE SALAD CREAM
2 hard-boiled egg yolks
1 tablespoon English mustard
juice of ½ lemon
pinch of caster sugar
2 tablespoons white wine vinegar
100ml double cream
100ml vegetable oil
sea salt and freshly ground black
    pepper

FOR THE VEGETABLE NAGE
25g butter
200g new potatoes, cooked and halved
100g fresh peas
100g broad beans, podded
a few mint leaves, chopped
a few sprigs of tarragon, chopped

Salad cream is not one of those recipes people expect to make, but whenever I do demos and show everyone how it easy it is to make your own, they go away and do it, as it tastes amazing, particularly with new potatoes.

To make the salad cream, put all the ingredients into a food processor and blitz until smooth. Pour into a small jug.

To make the vegetable nage, put 50ml water in a pan with the butter, then add the potatoes, peas and beans. Cook for 2–3 minutes, then stir through the herbs.

Pile the vegetables onto plates, tear over pieces of smoked salmon, scatter over the snipped chives and serve with the salad cream and lemon wedges.

POTATO AND SHRIMP BEIGNETS WITH LEMON MAYONNAISE

\

MAKES 20

FOR THE BEIGNETS
200ml water
85g butter
115g plain flour
2 eggs
pinch of salt
zest of 1 lemon
100g fresh brown shrimp
a few chives, chopped
150g potatoes, diced and cooked
vegetable oil, for coating spoon and
    deep-frying
sea salt and freshly ground black
    pepper

FOR THE LEMON MAYONNAISE
3 egg yolks
1 tablespoon Dijon mustard
200ml vegetable oil
zest and juice of 1 lemon

These beignets are so simple to make as they use a choux pastry base with a few extra ingredients, one of which I am obsessed with, and that's brown shrimp. The key to this dish is to have the oil at the right temperature; if the oil is too hot, the beignets can be quite doughy, and if too low, they can be quite greasy. A really simple snack.

To make the beignets, heat the water and butter in a pan over a gentle heat – do not let it boil. When the butter has melted, beat in the flour. Take off the heat and cool slightly, then beat in the eggs one at a time. Mix in the salt, lemon zest, brown shrimp, chives and diced potato and season.

Heat the oil in a deep-fat fryer or large pan to 170°C (340°F).

Dip a metal tablespoon in oil, then into the potato mixture and drop dollops into the hot oil. Cook for 4–5 minutes until golden brown and drain onto kitchen paper. You will need to do this in batches, repeating to use up all the mixture.

To make the lemon mayonnaise, whisk the egg yolks and mustard in a bowl. Slowly drizzle in the oil, whisking continuously. Season and add the lemon zest and juice. Serve with the potato and shrimp beignets.

SWEET POTATO, ROASTED RED PEPPER AND TOMATO SOUP

\

SERVES 4

2 sweet potatoes, peeled and diced
2 red peppers, core removed, cut into 8
1 shallot, diced
500g ripe tomatoes, halved
4 garlic cloves
1 red chilli, sliced
50ml olive oil
500ml warm vegetable stock
sea salt and freshly ground black
  pepper

TO SERVE (OPTIONAL)
drizzle of herb oil
drizzle of cream

When you are making soup, a lot of the time the tendency is to boil the ingredients, so by roasting the red pepper and tomatoes here, you get a very different flavour and one that works really well.

Preheat the oven to 200°C (180°C fan)/400°F/gas 6.

Place the sweet potatoes, peppers, shallot, tomatoes, garlic and chilli on a baking tray. Drizzle over the olive oil, season and roast for 40 minutes.

Carefully tip the roasted ingredients into a food processor, then add the warm stock and blitz until smooth. Pop into a pan and warm through.

Spoon the soup into bowls and drizzle with oil and cream, if you like.

SMOKED HADDOCK AND JERSEY ROYAL QUICHE

\

SERVES 6-8

FOR THE SHORTCRUST PASTRY

200g plain flour, plus extra for dusting

100g cold butter, cubed, plus extra for greasing

1 teaspoon salt

1 egg

FOR THE FILLING

2 onions, sliced

knob of butter

300g cooked Jersey Royals

400g smoked haddock, skinned and cut into chunks

75g Gruyère, grated

I love quiche, but I love it even more if it's served at room temperature or warm straight out of the oven. For me, the key is to always make the pastry by hand, that way it will be light and dissolve in your mouth, but the filling also needs egg yolks to keep the mixture nice and smooth and not solid.

Preheat the oven to 180°C (160°C fan)/350°F/gas 4.

Place the flour in a bowl, add the butter and salt, then rub between your fingers until the mixture looks like coarse breadcrumbs. Add the egg and mix in with your fingers, adding a little water if needed to bring the dough together. Knead on a floured surface until smooth, wrap in clingfilm and chill in the fridge for 30 minutes.

Grease a 24cm tart tin with butter. Dust a work surface with flour, roll out the pastry and use it to line the tin. Cover the pastry with clingfilm, fill it with flour and blind bake for 15–20 minutes. Remove from the oven and set aside.

To make the filling, sweat the onions in a pan with a knob of butter until deeply coloured, cool, then spread over the bottom of the tart case. Top with the potatoes and haddock.

FOR THE CUSTARD
3 eggs
3 egg yolks
150ml double cream
150ml full-fat milk
sea salt and freshly ground black
  pepper

FOR THE SALAD
600g mixed Isle of Wight tomatoes
50ml olive oil
15ml sherry vinegar

To make the custard, whisk together the eggs and egg yolks, cream and milk, then season.

Pour the custard into the filled pastry case, sprinkle the cheese over the top and bake in the oven for 40–50 minutes; the quiche should have a slight wobble in the middle when it is cooked. Remove the quiche from the oven and allow to sit for 5 minutes, then trim the edge of the pastry crust.

For the salad, slice the tomatoes into halves and quarters. Mix with the oil and vinegar and season.

Serve the quiche hot, warm or cold with the salad alongside.

TARTIFLETTE

\

SERVES 6

500g Anya potatoes
50g butter
125g lardons
2 red onions, finely sliced
3 garlic cloves, crushed
75ml dry white wine
120ml double cream
500g Reblochon, sliced
sea salt and freshly ground black
    pepper

This classic dish comes from Savoy in the French Alps, and it's often served to skiers. I don't do skiing – the thought of flying down a hill on two planks of wood just doesn't float my boat – but having said that, this dish is bloody delicious. You must use Reblochon cheese, which can be identified by the small green dot in the centre of the whole cheese.

Preheat the oven to 200°C (180°C fan)/400°F/gas 6.

Cook the potatoes in boiling salted water for 15–20 minutes. Drain, leave to cool and then slice.

Melt the butter in a flameproof, round ceramic dish and fry the potatoes for 5–8 minutes until crisp. Remove and set aside. Add the lardons to the dish and fry for a few minutes, then add the onions and garlic and sauté for 5 minutes. Season, then deglaze the dish with the wine and pour in the double cream.

Remove the dish from the heat and layer the onion and lardon mixture with the potatoes and Reblochon. Bake in the oven for 30 minutes.

MAINS

ARBROATH SMOKIE CAKES WITH CHILLI JAM

\

SERVES 4

FOR THE CAKES

110g Arbroath smokies, flesh flaked
110g mashed potato
1 red chilli, finely chopped
1 teaspoon medium curry powder
juice of 1 lime
vegetable oil, for deep-frying
75g plain flour, seasoned
2 eggs, beaten
90g panko breadcrumbs
sea salt and freshly ground black
   pepper

This amazing smoked haddock has such a vast history, coming from a small fishing village a few miles from Arbroath. There are so many legends about its origins, such as a fire destroying barrels of haddock in salt, but whatever happened, this is one of my favourite ingredients in the world. You can buy Arbroath smokies online, but for me the best chap who sells them is Iain Spink. Honestly, order some and whether you make this dish, simply smother the haddock with butter or warm through in the oven in newspaper, and you will see what I mean.

Mix the Arbroath smokies, mashed potato, chilli and curry powder in a bowl until well combined. Season with salt and pepper and lime juice, to taste. Divide the mixture into balls, about 2cm diameter.

Place the flour in one bowl, the beaten eggs in a second and the breadcrumbs in a third. Dredge each ball first in the flour, then dip it in the beaten egg, then roll it in the breadcrumbs until completely coated.

Carefully lower the Arbroath smokie cakes into the hot oil and fry for 3–4 minutes, or until crisp, golden brown and completely cooked through. Remove from the pan using a slotted spoon and drain onto kitchen paper. Keep warm until needed.

FOR THE CHILLI JAM

75g caster sugar
2 red chillies, roughly chopped
3 plum tomatoes, roughly chopped
8 lime leaves
2 lemongrass stems, tough outer leaves
    removed, finely chopped
25g fresh ginger, roughly chopped
2 garlic cloves
2 small shallots, roughly chopped
4 tablespoons Thai fish sauce (nam pla)
40ml sesame oil
50ml dark soy sauce
2 tablespoons clear honey
zest and juice of 3 limes
110g crème fraîche

To make the chilli jam, heat the sugar in a heavy-based saucepan over a low-medium heat until it melts and forms a golden-brown caramel. Do not stir and keep an eye on it so that it doesn't burn.

Blend all of the remaining chilli jam ingredients, except the crème fraîche, to a smooth purée in a food processor.

Once the sugar has caramelised, pour in the puréed chilli jam mixture and stir well. Bring the mixture to the boil, then reduce the heat and simmer for 4–5 minutes, or until sticky and jam-like. Remove from the heat and set aside to cool. Once the chilli jam mixture has cooled, stir in the crème fraîche until well combined.

To serve, pop the cakes onto small skewers and place onto a serving plate. Spoon the chilli jam into a bowl and serve alongside the cakes.

PORK AND APPLE FAGGOT WITH BURNT BRAMLEY APPLE PURÉE AND POTATO PURÉE

\

SERVES 10

FOR THE POTATO PURÉE
12 rooster potatoes
250g butter
200ml double cream

FOR THE BURNT BRAMLEY APPLE PURÉE
1kg Bramley apples, unpeeled and
 diced
150ml cider

FOR THE PORK AND APPLE FAGGOT
1kg minced pork belly
350g minced pork liver
750g minced pork shoulder
4 shallots, minced
2 garlic cloves, minced
650g burnt Bramley apple purée
1 red chilli
1 teaspoon mace
1 teaspoon chopped sage
1 teaspoon chopped thyme
1 teaspoon chopped parsley
1 teaspoon cumin seeds, toasted
1 teaspoon coriander seeds, toasted
150g oats
fine sea salt and freshly ground black
pepper

This isn't one of my dishes but comes courtesy of Dougie Crampton, who has been with me for nigh on 12 years and runs my Manchester restaurant. He is a bloody legend, and this dish is one of the many reasons why it is so busy.

Preheat the oven to 180°C (160°C fan)/350°F/gas 4.

To make the potato purée, pop the potatoes on a baking tray, prick all over with a fork, then bake for 1¼ hours. Remove from the oven, scoop out the flesh and pass it a drum sieve into a bowl. Combine with the butter and cream to make a loose purée and gently warm through in a saucepan over a low heat.

To make the apple purée, place the diced apple on a non-stick baking tray and roast for 30 minutes until soft and caramelised. Remove from the oven and deglaze the pan with the cider on the hob. Transfer the mixture to a food processor and blitz until smooth. Chill in the fridge until needed.

To make the faggot, increase the oven temperature to 200°C (180°C fan)/400°F/gas 6. Combine all the ingredients, except the oats, and season to taste. Coat the faggot in the oats and seal in a hot pan for 2 minutes on each side, then transfer to non-stick baking tray and roast in the oven for 15 minutes.

FOR THE CIDER GLAZE
1 tablespoon vegetable oil
5 shallots, sliced
2 garlic cloves, sliced
a few sprigs of thyme
4 x 750ml bottles Welsh Mountain
    Cider
2 litres reduced roast chicken stock
1 tablespoon wholegrain mustard
maple syrup, to taste
potato starch (optional)

TO SERVE
1 apple, cut into matchsticks
crispy sage leaves

To make the cider glaze, add the oil to a pan, then sweat the shallots, garlic and thyme until caramelised. Deglaze the pan with the cider and cook until it has reduced by half. Add the reduced roast chicken stock, wholegrain mustard and maple syrup and continue to cook to warm through. Thicken with a little potato starch to a glaze-like consistency if needed.

To serve, spoon the potato purée onto plates and top with a slice of faggot. Spoon over the apple sauce and then pour over the cider glaze. Scatter over some pieces of apple and sage leaves to finish.

BEER CAN CHICKEN WITH TRAY-BAKED GARLIC AND LEMON VEGETABLES

\

SERVES 6

1 large chicken (about 1.8kg)
olive oil, for rubbing
330ml can of lager

FOR THE DRY RUB
4 tablespoons fine salt
3 tablespoons light brown sugar
2 tablespoons sweet smoked paprika
1 teaspoon cayenne pepper
1 teaspoon onion powder
1 teaspoon garlic powder
1 teaspoon English mustard powder

FOR THE TRAY-BAKED
VEGETABLES
250g new potatoes, halved
3 carrots, cut into large chunks
2 red onions, halved
1 spring cabbage, halved
1 lemon, halved
1 bulb of garlic, halved
1 sprig of rosemary
extra virgin olive oil, for drizzling
sea salt and freshly ground black
   pepper

If your BBQ is big enough, i.e. it has a lid, you can try cooking this dish in it; if not, it works well in the oven, and although it might look a bit odd it doesn't taste odd. Make sure you use a tall can of lager for a bigger chicken or try cider instead.

To make the dry rub, mix all the ingredients together and store any leftovers in an airtight container.

Preheat the oven to 200°C (180°C fan)/400°F/gas 6.

Place all the vegetables, lemon, garlic and rosemary in a roasting tray and season.

Slash the chicken and remove the wish bone. Rub the chicken all over with olive oil and then cover completely with the dry rub. Place over the opened beer can, set on top of the vegetables and roast for 1½ hours.

Remove the tray from the oven, carefully remove the chicken from the can and place on a platter. Squeeze the juice from the roasted lemon halves over the vegetables and the roasted garlic cloves out of their skins. Pile the vegetables around the chicken, drizzle over some olive oil and serve.

BEER CAN CHICKEN WITH
GARLIC ROSEMARY POTATOES

\

SERVES 4

1 bulb of garlic
2 red onions, cut into eighths
1 bunch of rosemary
50ml olive oil, plus extra for the
　　potatoes
400g new potatoes
sea salt and freshly ground black
　　pepper

FOR THE CHICKEN
1 large chicken (about 1.8kg)
1 bulb of garlic
1 small bunch of rosemary
330ml can IPA

This dish is as popular in our house as it is on TV. The recipe uses a BBQ to cook the chicken and, when hot, the beer bubbles and steams the chicken from the inside out. On a recent trip to America I found that a lot of people were cooking dishes like this at tailgate meets, which are BBQ feasts before college football games.

Heat a BBQ with a lid until hot and the coals are white.

Slash the chicken, remove the wish bone and fill the cavity with the garlic and rosemary. Place the chicken over the opened beer can and transfer to a roasting tray. Scatter around the garlic, onions and rosemary and drizzle with the oil. Pop on the BBQ, shut the lid and cook for 45 minutes–1 hour. Wrap the potatoes in foil, drizzle with oil and cook alongside the chicken.

To serve, carefully remove the can from the chicken, place the chicken, onions and rosemary onto a platter and serve with the potatoes.

BUNNY CHOW

\

SERVES 4

2 tablespoons vegetable oil
½ teaspoon cumin seeds
½ teaspoon fennel seeds
2.5cm piece of cinnamon stick
2 green cardamom pods
1 star anise
1 bay leaf
1 onion, finely chopped
2 tablespoons curry powder
2 tomatoes, chopped
1kg boneless leg of lamb, cut into 1cm
  dice
1 tablespoon finely chopped fresh
  ginger
1 tablespoon finely chopped garlic
10–12 curry leaves
2 large potatoes, cut into cubes the
  same size as the meat
2 tablespoons finely chopped coriander
  leaves
2 tablespoons lime juice
2 loaves of white bread, unsliced, tops
  and most of the crumbs removed
sea salt
coriander leaves, to garnish

I first came across this recipe made properly by one of the best Indian chefs in the UK, Atul Kochhar, who explained that it's sort of like a fast-food dish. I have had various different versions of bunny chow, including from South Africa, and the dish seems to have been created for occasions when there's no traditional roti or rice.

Heat the oil in a pan and sauté the whole spices and bay leaf until the spices sizzle. Add the onion and cook for 5–7 minutes until translucent. Stir in the curry powder and sauté for 1 minute, then add the tomatoes and stir to mix. Cook over a medium heat, stirring often, until sauce-like.

Add the lamb, ginger, garlic and curry leaves, bring to the boil, then reduce the heat and simmer, stirring occasionally, for 40–50 minutes or until the meat is tender.

Add the potatoes, salt to taste and 200ml water. Continue simmering for 12–15 minutes until the meat and potatoes are perfectly cooked. Stir in the chopped coriander and lime juice.

To serve, spoon the meat and potato mixture into the hollows in the bread and garnish with coriander leaves.

BBQ LAMB WITH CHIMICHURRI SAUCE AND NEW POTATOES

\

SERVES 4

400g new potatoes, blanched
25g butter
a few sprigs of coriander
1 leg of lamb, deboned and butterflied
a few sprigs of rosemary
sea salt and freshly ground black
    pepper

FOR THE CHIMICHURRI SAUCE
15g Vietnamese coriander, chopped
15g coriander, chopped
15g mint, chopped
2 garlic cloves, chopped
1 green chilli, chopped
½ shallot, chopped
25ml red wine vinegar
juice of 2 limes
50ml olive oil

If you're sick of pesto, then chimichurri is a brilliant alternative, especially with grilled meats on the BBQ. The key is to use plenty of fresh herbs, and the vinegar is just as important as the lime. Chimichurri is also wonderful with simple BBQ roast vegetables for a vegetarian alternative.

Heat a BBQ until the coals are grey.

Wrap the potatoes, butter and coriander in foil. Season the lamb and sprinkle with rosemary. Put the lamb on the BBQ and cook for 15 minutes on each side, adding the potatoes in foil when you turn the lamb over.

To make the sauce, mix the herbs and garlic together in a pestle and mortar and stir through the chilli and shallot. Stir in the vinegar, lime juice and olive oil. Season.

To serve, pile the lamb and potatoes onto a platter and top with the sauce.

BEEF CHEEKS WITH MASH AND CARROTS

\

SERVES 4

2kg beef cheeks
2 tablespoons plain flour
2 tablespoons olive oil
25g butter
250ml Burgundy red wine
75ml brandy
500ml beef stock
1 shallot, finely chopped
1 onion, sliced
1 garlic clove, crushed
1 leek, sliced
1 carrot, chopped
2 sprigs of thyme
2 sprigs of flat-leaf parsley
sea salt and freshly ground black
    pepper

FOR THE CARROTS
1 bunch of carrots, peeled
4 star anise
50g butter
50g caster sugar

FOR THE MASH
1kg floury potatoes, peeled and
    cut into chunks
100g butter
100ml double cream

Various different types of meat and more unusual cuts are becoming more widely available, which is brilliant. Beef cheeks are an amazing choice to braise in the winter months, when we use about 1,000 kilos a week! The longer you cook them, the better they get.

To make the beef cheeks, toss the beef with the flour and season with salt and black pepper.

Heat a large sauté pan until hot, splash in the olive oil and butter, add the beef and fry until browned on each side. Pop into a large casserole pan.

Add the red wine, brandy and beef stock to a pan and bring to a simmer, then pour over the meat and add the rest of the ingredients. Cover and cook over a low heat for 4 hours until the beef cheeks are tender and the sauce has just thickened.

For the carrots, put all the ingredients in a pan, add water to just cover, bring to the boil, then simmer for 30 minutes.

Meanwhile, to make the mash, put the potatoes in a pan of salted water and bring to the boil. Reduce the heat and simmer for 12–15 minutes until the potatoes are tender.

Drain and return the potatoes to the pan, then place over the heat for a minute to dry off any excess moisture. Mash well, then add the butter and cream, beating to form a smooth mash. Season with salt and black pepper.

To serve, pile some mash onto each plate, spoon over a generous portion of beef cheeks with the carrots alongside.

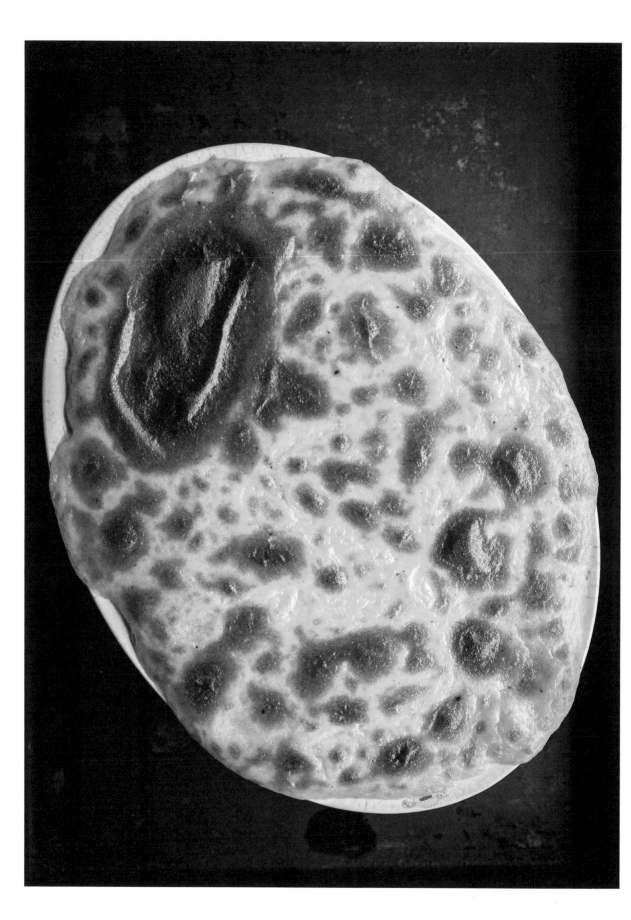

CHEESY POTATO AND BEEF PIE

\

SERVES 6–8

1 onion, sliced
25g butter
700g minced beef
2 tablespoons Worcestershire sauce
500ml beef stock
1 large bunch of parsley, chopped
sea salt and freshly ground black
    pepper

FOR THE RAREBIT
400g Cheddar, grated
50ml Welsh beer
a few drops of Tabasco sauce
1 tablespoon Worcestershire sauce
1 tablespoon English mustard
1 tablespoon plain flour
1 egg yolk

FOR THE MASHED POTATO
50g butter
100ml double cream
1kg mashed potato

TO SERVE
frozen peas

Think of a cottage pie on steroids and this is what you get. The Welsh rarebit can be made in advance, and either use it in this dish or on toast or smoked haddock.

In a frying pan over a medium heat, fry the onion in the butter for 10 minutes, then add the beef. Cook until coloured, then add the Worcestershire sauce and beef stock and cook over a high heat for 20 minutes. Add the parsley and season.

To make the rarebit, put the cheese in a large pan, add the beer, Tabasco, Worcestershire sauce and mustard. Warm through gently until all the cheese has melted.

When all the cheese is melted, stir in the flour and gently cook it for another minute or two. Season, add the egg yolk and beat together. Remove from the heat and set aside.

For the mashed potato, melt the butter and cream in a large pan, season and add the mashed potato. Beat together and warm through gently.

Preheat the grill to high.

Spoon the beef into a 20 x 15cm ovenproof dish and top with the mashed potato, then the rarebit. Pop under the grill for 5 minutes until golden and bubbling.

Meanwhile, cook the peas in boiling water, then drain and serve with the pie.

BBQ PORK RIBS WITH SLAW AND JACKET POTATOES

\

SERVES 4

4 baking potatoes
2 x pork rib rack
1 onion
1 carrot
a few black peppercorns
1 bay leaf
1 teaspoon smoked paprika
1 teaspoon chilli powder
2 tablespoons salt
2 tablespoons caster sugar

FOR THE SLAW
1 carrot, peeled and julienned
½ mooli, julienned
¼ red cabbage, thinly sliced
1 red onion, sliced
1 small bunch of coriander, chopped
mayo, to bind
sea salt and freshly ground black
   pepper

FOR THE SAUCE
250ml tomato ketchup
25ml white vinegar
100g soft brown sugar
1 garlic clove, minced
80ml dark soy sauce
100ml maple syrup

TO SERVE
butter
crème fraîche
chives
crispy onions

This is one of the first ideas I had when I got involved with SpudULike – slow-cooked ribs with a nice slaw, served with beautifully cooked, fluffy jacket potatoes. For me, Marabel are the best baking potatoes you will find. At SpudULike we just prick them with a fork and cook them for 1 hour 20 minutes – no oil, no salt, just beautiful crispy skin and a creamy, buttery texture.

Preheat the oven to 180°C (160°C fan)/350°F/gas 4.

Prick the potatoes all over with a fork, pop onto a baking tray and bake for 50 minutes. Increase the temperature to 200°C (180°C fan)/400°F/gas 6 and bake for a further 30 minutes.

Place the ribs, onion, carrot, peppercorns, bay, leaf, spices, salt and sugar in a large pan and add enough water to cover. Bring to the boil, then simmer for 1 hour, until tender. Remove the ribs from the saucepan and place onto a baking tray to cool.

Place all the sauce ingredients in a small pan, bring to the boil, then simmer gently for 5 minutes until thickened. Use to brush liberally over the ribs, then place in the oven and roast for 15–20 minutes, glazing with more sauce halfway through.

Meanwhile, make the slaw. Mix together the carrot, mooli, cabbage, onion and coriander in a bowl, adding enough mayo to combine, then season.

To serve, split the potatoes, top with butter and slaw, then top with the ribs. Dollop on crème fraîche and sprinkle over chives and crispy onions.

CLUB SANDWICH AND CHIPS

\

SERVES 1

3 tomatoes
a few sprigs of thyme
100g butter
12 slices of pancetta
3 slices of sourdough bread
6 slices of Gruyère
100g cooked chicken
2 thick slices of ham

FOR THE CHIPS
vegetable oil, for deep-frying
2 Chippies Choice potatoes, peeled and
  cut into matchsticks
sea salt and freshly ground black
  pepper

FOR THE MAYO
3 egg yolks
1 tablespoon Dijon mustard
200ml vegetable oil

I find the best club sandwich is always served with fries and proper mayonnaise, which makes it taste so much better.

Preheat the oven to 170°C (150°C fan)/340°F/gas 3½.

Slice the tomatoes in half horizontally, pop onto a baking tray, then season, sprinkle with the thyme, dot with butter and bake for 1 hour.

Heat the vegetable oil in deep-fat fryer or large pan to 180°C (350°F).

Fry the chips until crisp and golden, drain and season.

Meanwhile, make the mayo by blitzing the egg yolks and Dijon mustard together in a food processor. Slowly drizzle in the oil until thick. Season.

To make the sarnie, fry the pancetta in a frying pan until crisp. Place one slice of sourdough on a plate. Layer up with half the pancetta, Gruyère, chicken, ham, tomatoes and lots of mayo. Top with a slice of sourdough. Add the remaining pancetta, Gruyère, chicken and ham with the remaining tomatoes and some mayo and top with the final slice of bread.

Serve the sarnie with the chips on the side and extra mayo.

CHICKEN AND WAFFLES

\

SERVES 4

2kg whole chicken, portioned into 8–10 portions
25ml olive oil
25g butter
100g bacon lardons
1 shallot, diced
2 tablespoons tomato purée
200g chestnut mushrooms
200ml French white wine
400ml chicken stock
1 small bunch of tarragon, leaves picked
sea salt and freshly ground black pepper

FOR THE WAFFLES
250g plain flour
1 teaspoon baking powder
1 teaspoon caster sugar
3 eggs
200ml full-fat milk
2 tablespoons chopped spring onions
100g potatoes, peeled, diced and blanched
2 tomatoes, skinned, deseeded and finely chopped

This is a simplified version of a dish made by one of the best chefs in the world, Thomas Keller, when he appeared on my TV show – the list of his ingredients wouldn't fit on one page, and nor would his method... Think of this recipe as a bit like a chicken chasseur.

Preheat the oven to 180°C (160°C fan)/350°F/gas 4.

Fry the chicken in the oil and butter in a casserole pan until it is coloured, then season. Add the bacon, shallot, tomato purée and mushrooms and cook for 2 minutes.

Add the wine and bring it to the boil, then add the stock and half the tarragon. Cook in the oven for 45 minutes. Remove from the oven and sprinkle over the remaining tarragon.

Heat a waffle machine to high, following the manufacturer's instructions.

To make the waffles, whisk all the ingredients together, then ladle the batter into the waffle machine and cook until golden.

To serve, pop the waffles and chicken onto plates, then spoon over some of the sauce.

CHICKEN KYIV WITH WILD GARLIC AND BUTTERED JERSEY ROYALS

\

SERVES 2

225g butter
7 garlic cloves, crushed
1 small bunch of wild garlic, chopped
1 small bunch of parsley, chopped
2 French-trimmed chicken breasts, cut in half
75g plain flour, seasoned
2 eggs, beaten
100g panko breadcrumbs
vegetable oil, for shallow-frying
200g Jersey Royals
sea salt and freshly ground black pepper

The important thing with this recipe is to make sure the chicken is cooked through; if you are doing this in a frying pan, make sure you have plenty of oil, about 1cm, and keep the chicken moving around in the pan. Then, once coloured, you can finish it off in the oven, if you like. Traditionally the chicken would be deep-fried at about 160°C (140°C fan)/325°F/gas 3 for 10–12 minutes, so you can cook it like this if you prefer.

Mix 200g of the butter, the garlic, half the wild garlic and half the parsley together, then season.

Remove the skin and bones from the chicken. Cut a hole all the way through the chicken breast from the top almost to the bottom and remove a small piece of chicken. Fill with the butter and seal with the small piece of chicken.

Place the flour in one bowl, the beaten eggs in a second and the breadcrumbs in a third.

Dip each chicken fillet parcel in flour, then egg, then flour and egg again, and then dip into the breadcrumbs.

Add some oil to a frying pan and shallow-fry the chicken for 10–12 minutes until cooked through and golden brown. Drain onto kitchen paper, then season with salt.

Meanwhile, cook the potatoes in boiling salted water for 12 minutes. Drain, return to the pan, season and add the remaining butter.

To serve, spoon the potatoes into the centre of each plate and top with a chicken Kyiv.

CASTERBRIDGE CÔTE DE BOEUF WITH CAVOLO NERO AND GNOCCHI, WILD MUSHROOM AND BONE MARROW GRATIN

\

SERVES 4

FOR THE CÔTE DE BOEUF
2 x 700g côte de boeuf
1 teaspoon olive oil
sea salt and freshly ground black
  pepper

FOR THE GNOCCHI
900g hot mashed potato (oven-baked
  and passed through a drum)
20g plain flour, plus extra for dusting
6 egg yolks
4g sea salt

FOR THE BONE MARROW CRUST
30g bone marrow
30g butter
300g brioche breadcrumbs

FOR THE GRATIN
50g butter
50g plain flour
1.5 litres full-fat milk
1 shallot, thickly sliced
1 bay leaf
4 black peppercorns
1 clove
1 teaspoon olive oil
300g mixed wild mushrooms
3 tablespoons finely chopped chervil

We serve this gratin in the restaurant and it's one of the most popular side dishes with a simple steak. You can make the gnocchi in advance and simply freeze it, but the combination of bone marrow with the crust makes it a great accompaniment to beef.

Preheat the oven to 200°C (180°C fan)/400°F/gas 6.

To make the gnocchi, mix all the ingredients in a bowl while the potato is hot, without overworking the mix. Divide the mixture in half and then, on a floured surface, roll each piece into a long sausage shape, about 1.25cm in diameter. With a sharp knife, cut each sausage into 2.5cm gnocchi.

Bring a pan of salted water to the boil, add the gnocchi and blanch for 1–2 minutes. Drain and place onto an oiled tray in the fridge to chill.

To make the bone marrow crust, place the bone marrow and butter in a pan and heat until melted. Remove from the heat, add the brioche crumbs and mix well.

To make the gratin, begin by making a roux. Melt the butter in a pan, then add the flour, stirring continuously for 2–3 minutes to cook it out. Remove from the heat and set to one side to cool.

Infuse the milk by bringing it to the boil with the shallot, bay leaf, peppercorns and clove, then remove from the heat and let it sit for 20 minutes.

Pass the milk through a strainer into a saucepan and return to the heat to warm through. Add the cold roux to the hot milk and whisk. Bring to the boil, allow to boil for 2 minutes, then take off the heat.

FOR THE CAVOLO NERO
1 head of cavolo nero, leaves picked
   and stripped from centre stalk
50g butter
2 shallots, finely sliced

Meanwhile, heat a frying pan until hot, add the olive oil and the mushrooms and sauté for 1–2 minutes until just tender. Season with salt and black pepper.

Preheat the grill to high.

Place the gnocchi with the béchamel in an ovenproof dish, then add the cooked mushrooms and the chervil and toss everything together. Top with the bone marrow crust. Place on a baking sheet under the grill and heat until golden and bubbling.

To make the côte de boeuf, season the meat with salt and black pepper on both sides and rub with the olive oil. Heat a griddle pan until very hot, add the beef and sear on both sides for 1 minute until chargrilled.

Transfer the côte de boeuf to a roasting tray and roast in the oven for 8–10 minutes for rare. Remove from the oven and rest for at least 5 minutes.

Meanwhile, make the cavolo nero. Bring a pan of salted water to the boil. Add the cavolo nero and blanch for 30 seconds. Remove from the pan and drain well.

Heat a frying pan until hot, add the butter and heat until foaming, then add the shallots and cavolo nero and sauté for 1–2 minutes.

To serve, carve the côte de boeuf into slices and serve with a spoonful of the gnocchi gratin. Pile the cavolo nero to one side.

CRAB CAKES WITH KATSU CURRY SAUCE

\

MAKES 4

FOR THE CRAB CAKES
400g white crab meat
400g potatoes, peeled, cooked and
    riced
zest and juice of 1 lemon
1 egg yolk
25g plain flour for dusting
vegetable oil, for frying
sea salt and freshly ground black
    pepper

FOR THE KATSU CURRY SAUCE
15ml vegetable oil
100g onion paste
100g garlic paste
1 tablespoon mild curry powder
1 tablespoon ground cumin
1 tablespoon ground coriander
1 tablespoon ground turmeric
200ml chicken stock
20ml dark soy sauce

TO SERVE
micro coriander
sliced spring onions

This sauce comes from a good mate of mine, Gareth Ward, who runs one of the best restaurants in the country, Ynyshir, in Wales. It is without a doubt another of my favourite dishes in this book.

To make the crab cakes, mix together the crab, potato, lemon zest and juice and egg yolk, and season. Dust your hands with flour and form into four 8cm discs, 2cm deep.

Heat a non-stick frying pan, pour in some oil, then add the crab cakes and cook for 2–3 minutes on each side.

Meanwhile, make the sauce. Add the vegetable oil, onion and garlic pastes to a pan and fry for 5 minutes, then add the spices. Cook for another 2 minutes, then add the stock and soy sauce. Bring to the boil, then remove from the heat. Transfer to a food processor and blitz until smooth.

To serve, spoon the sauce onto plates, top with the crab cakes and sprinkle over the micro coriander and spring onions.

GRILLED PLAICE FILLETS WITH WARMED POTTED SHRIMP AND JERSEY ROYALS

\

SERVES 2

2 large plaice, heads removed, cut in
   half lengthways
50g butter
100g cooked Jersey Royals
100g asparagus tips
50g sugar snap peas
sea salt and freshly ground black
   pepper

FOR THE SAUCE
100g potted shrimp
½ teaspoon Gentleman's Relish
1 small bunch of parsley, chopped
juice of 1 lemon
100g frozen peas

TO SERVE
pea shoots
1 lemon, peeled and sliced

I get my fish from a wonderful chap called Johnny from Flying Fish Seafoods in Cornwall. What I love about this recipe is its simplicity – all the ingredients come from the UK, simply cooked and super tasty.

Pan-fry the plaice in half the butter for 6–8 minutes, turning halfway through, then season.

Steam the Jersey Royals, asparagus and sugar snap peas for 2–3 minutes.

To make the sauce, gently warm the potted shrimp with the relish and the remaining butter. Add the parsley, lemon juice and peas and season with black pepper.

To serve, pile the potatoes and veg onto a platter, top with the fish and spoon over the sauce. Top with pea shoots and lemon slices.

CHILLI JACKET POTATOES

\

SERVES 6

6 baking potatoes

FOR THE CHILLI
50ml vegetable oil
1kg beef stewing steak, diced
1 onion, diced
1 celery stick, diced
1 carrot, diced
2 garlic cloves, diced
2 chillies, diced
1 teaspoon ground coriander
1 teaspoon chilli powder
1 tablespoon smoked chipotle chilli
500ml passata
100ml beef stock
1 glass of red wine
2 tablespoons tomato purée
400g can kidney beans, washed and
    drained

TO SERVE
guacamole
fresh coriander, roughly chopped

This is a dish my home economist, Sam Head, created while we were working on this book. It was a favourite in her house, and then it was a hit in mine too.

To make the chilli, heat a large pan and add the oil. Fry the beef in batches until deeply coloured and browned. Add all the remaining ingredients, except the kidney beans, and simmer over a gentle heat for 4 hours. Stir through the beans and cook for a few more minutes to warm them through.

Meanwhile, preheat the oven to 200°C (180°C fan)/400°F/gas 6.

Pop the potatoes onto a baking tray, prick all over with a fork, then bake for 1¼ hours.

To serve, cut a cross in the top of each potato, spoon over the chilli, dot with guacamole and sprinkle over the coriander.

HADDOCK FISHCAKES AND MUSTARD SAUCE

\

SERVES 4

FOR THE FISHCAKES

600g haddock
1 litre full-fat milk
1 bay leaf
600g mashed potato
6 spring onions, sliced
1 small bunch of parsley, chopped
squeeze of lemon
100g plain flour, seasoned
2 eggs, beaten
100g panko breadcrumbs
vegetable oil, for shallow-frying
sea salt and freshly ground black
    pepper

FOR THE SAUCE

25g butter
1 tablespoon plain flour
50ml white wine
squeeze of lemon juice
1 tablespoon wholegrain mustard
1 teaspoon Dijon mustard
a few chives, chopped

FOR THE KALE

25g butter
1 bunch of kale, leaves stripped from
    the centre stalk

If there is one dish that evokes memories of food from my grandparents, it has to be this. My granddad dug potatoes from his allotment and made the classic mustard sauce using the poaching liquor. Bloody wonderful.

Add the haddock, milk and bay leaf to a pan and poach for 3–4 minutes. Drain and cool, retaining the milk for the sauce.

Mix the mashed potato, cooked haddock, spring onions, parsley and lemon juice together. Gently form into 4 patties.

Place the flour in one bowl, the beaten eggs in a second and the breadcrumbs in a third.

Dip each patty first in the flour, then in the beaten egg, then in the breadcrumbs. Add to the oil and fry for 2–3 minutes on each side.

To make the sauce, heat the butter. When foaming, whisk in the flour, then whisk in the reserved milk, wine, lemon juice and both mustards. Season and mix in the chives.

Heat a pan with a splash of water, add the butter, then the kale and cook for 2 minutes; all the liquid should evaporate.

To serve, pop the kale onto plates, top each with a fishcake and drizzle round the mustard sauce.

DHAL WITH POTATOES AND SPINACH

\
SERVES 4

80g butter
1 onion, diced
5cm piece fresh ginger, chopped
3 garlic cloves, chopped
2 teaspoons black mustard seeds
1½ teaspoons ground turmeric
2 teaspoons ground coriander
2 teaspoons garam masala
250g yellow split peas, soaked
   overnight in cold water and drained
400g cooked new potatoes
240g baby spinach
sea salt and freshly ground black
   pepper

TO SERVE
handful of coriander, roughly chopped
handful of mint, leaves picked and
   roughly chopped

There are so many versions of dhal, but over the years, this has become one of my favourites. The yellow split peas must be soaked overnight, and this dish is super-tasty served on its own as well as with added prawns or chicken. It's also great served alongside fish if you want to bulk it out.

Melt half the butter in a large saucepan over a medium–high heat. Add the onion and fry, stirring regularly, for about 10 minutes, or until soft and golden.

Stir in the ginger and garlic and fry for another minute, then add the mustard seeds, turmeric, coriander and garam masala. Season well and cook the spices for 1–2 minutes, then add the split peas and 850ml water.

Reduce the heat to a simmer and cook the split peas for 30 minutes until tender. You may have to add a little more water, depending on how large your pan is. Add the potatoes and cook until warmed through. Finish by stirring through the spinach and the remaining butter.

To serve, sprinkle with the herbs.

FISH AND CHIPS WITH MUSHY PEAS AND TARTARE SAUCE

\

SERVES 2

300g skinless cod fillet, sliced in half
vegetable oil, for frying

FOR THE MUSHY PEAS
200g marrowfat peas
1 tablespoon baking powder
½ teaspoon caster sugar
25g butter
sea salt and freshly ground black
   pepper

FOR THE CHIPS
4 large potatoes, peeled and thickly cut
   into lengths
vegetable oil, for deep-frying

FOR THE BATTER
250g gluten-free self-raising flour
350ml cider
1 teaspoon white wine vinegar

FOR THE TARTARE SAUCE
3 egg yolks
1 tablespoons Dijon mustard
200ml vegetable oil
squeeze of lemon juice
1 tablespoon white wine vinegar
½ shallot, finely diced
4 small gherkins, diced
1 teaspoon small capers
a few sprigs of dill and parsley,
   chopped

This comes from two ends of the country – down south from Nathan Outlaw, who showed me this batter (and I have used it ever since), and the Magpie Café in Whitby, which to my mind serves some of the best fish and chips in the UK.

Put the peas and baking powder in a bowl, cover with cold water and soak overnight in the fridge. Drain and rinse the peas, then place in a pan. Cover with cold water and bring to the boil, then simmer for 30 minutes, season and stir through the sugar and butter.

To make the chips, blanch the potatoes in a pan of boiling water for 5 minutes, then drain and tip onto a baking tray lined with kitchen paper.

Meanwhile, heat the vegetable oil in a deep-fat fryer or large pan to 170°C (340°F).

Add the potatoes to the hot oil and fry for 8–10 minutes until crisp. Drain onto kitchen paper.

Whisk all the ingredients together for the batter. Dip both fish portions in the batter and fry individually for 6–8 minutes, then drain onto kitchen paper.

To make the tartare sauce, blitz the egg yolks and mustard in a food processor, slowly drizzling in the oil. Spoon into a bowl, mix in all the remaining ingredients and season.

To serve, spoon the sauce onto plates and top with the fish, chips and a spoonful of mushy peas.

RACLETTE

\

SERVES 8

1kg Raclette cheese, sliced

TO SERVE
boiled new potatoes
mixed cold meats
pickled onions
gherkins
1 endive, leaves separated
1 baguette, sliced

We often make this as a nice special outside the fire pit of the restaurant when the weather is drawing in. No snow and skis, but it kinda works.

Set up and turn on a raclette grill following the manufacturer's instructions. Heat the slices of cheese on the grill until melted.

Alternatively, preheat a grill to hot or the oven to 200°C (180°C fan)/400°F/gas 6, place the cheese slices in an ovenproof dish and cook until bubbling.

Serve hot with all the accompaniments.

POTATO PIE WITH SARDINES AND CHUTNEY

\

SERVES 6

FOR THE PIE

25ml vegetable oil

25g butter

½ teaspoon ground cumin

½ teaspoon ground coriander

4 large potatoes, peeled and thinly sliced

12 sardines, gutted and scaled

125g bacon lardons

olive oil, for drizzling

sea salt and freshly ground black pepper

FOR THE CHUTNEY

2 apples, cored and chopped

2 pears, cored and chopped

1 teaspoon medium curry powder

1 shallot, finely chopped

5cm piece of fresh ginger, grated

2 garlic cloves, grated

TO SERVE

handful of coriander, chopped

Sardines are one of the real seasonal treats we look forward to at the restaurant in the summer when the shoals of sardines come in to feed, and are quickly followed by large predators around the coastline as well. Sardines simply cooked with potatoes like this taste amazing... proper grub!

Preheat the oven to 200°C (180°C fan)/400°F/gas 6.

To make the chutney, pop the apples, pears and curry powder into a large saucepan and add 100ml water. Bring to the boil, then add the shallot, ginger and garlic and cook for 5 minutes. Remove from the heat and set aside to cool.

To make the pie, heat a large, ovenproof, non-stick frying pan and add the oil, butter and ground cumin and coriander. When foaming, take off the heat and layer up the potatoes to cover the base. Pop back on the heat and cook until the potatoes are crisp. Lay the sardines over the potato base and sprinkle with bacon. Drizzle with olive oil and season, then bake in the oven for 15–20 minutes.

To serve, tip the pie onto a board (so that the potatoes are on top) and dot with the chutney, then sprinkle over the chopped coriander.

FISHERMAN'S PIE

\

SERVES 6

450g haddock, skin removed
450g cod, skin removed
12 scallops
24 prawns, peeled and deveined
2 Arbroath smokies (optional)
500ml full-fat milk
2 bay leaves
½ onion, studded with 4 cloves
40g butter
2½ tablespoons plain flour
1 small bunch of parsley, chopped

FOR THE TOPPING
800g mashed potato
50g butter, melted
100ml double cream

TO SERVE
600g frozen peas
knob of butter

The great thing about fish pie is that you can make it a few days in advance and cook it when required, plus it freezes quite well. Whatever fish you use, I always like to add smoked haddock in some form to give the pie a depth of flavour.

Preheat the oven to 200°C (180°C fan)/400°F/gas 6.

Cut the haddock and cod into large chunks, pop into an ovenproof dish and top with the scallops, prawns and flakes of Arbroath smokies, if using.

Add the milk, bay leaves and onion studded with the cloves to a pan and heat through gently for 2 minutes. Remove and discard the bay leaves and onion.

To make the white sauce, melt the butter in a pan, whisk in the flour and cook out for 2 minutes. Add the milk and whisk, simmering until bubbling. Stir in the parsley.

Cover the fish with the sauce. Mix the mashed potato with the butter and cream and dollop over the top of the fish, spreading to cover the whole pie. Bake for 30–40 minutes until golden brown and bubbling.

Meanwhile, add the peas to a pan of boiling salted water and cook for 2 minutes. Drain, return to the pan and stir through the butter to melt. Serve with the fish pie.

HASH WITH MAPLE SYRUP, PANCETTA AND FRIED EGGS

\

12 slices of pancetta
drizzle of vegetable oil
2 eggs

FOR THE HASH
1 large potato, peeled, cooked and
    diced
25g butter
15ml olive oil
sea salt and freshly ground black
    pepper

TO SERVE
maple syrup

This is a stereotypical chefs' breakfast, especially if the entire brigade is set for a big day ahead, as it's simple, quick to make and super tasty. It can be made with any type of potatoes you have to hand.

Heat a frying pan over a high heat and fry the pancetta until crisp. Remove from the pan.

For the hash, pop the potato into the frying pan with the butter and oil, season, and cook for 2–3 minutes until golden. Flip over and crush lightly with a potato masher.

Heat a separate frying pan and add a drizzle of oil, then break in the eggs and fry until crisp.

To serve, spoon the hash onto plates, top with the pancetta and eggs and drizzle over maple syrup.

HOMEMADE BAKED BEANS AND CHEESY JACKET POTATOES

\

SERVES 4

4 baking potatoes
100g butter
200g Cheddar, grated

FOR THE BAKED BEANS
25ml butter
25ml olive oil
200g bacon lardons
1 tablespoon smoked paprika
2 tablespoons dark brown sugar
1 teaspoon English mustard powder
400g can haricot beans, rinsed and
   drained
300ml passata
1 small bunch of flat-leaf parsley,
   chopped
sea salt and freshly ground black
   pepper

When I bought SpudULike, this was the most popular topping – and it still is! You can try all sorts of different baked potato toppings, but beans and cheese is what everyone loves. I don't blame them.

Preheat the oven to 200°C (180°C fan)/400°F/gas 6.

Pop the potatoes onto a baking tray, prick all over with a fork, then bake for 1¼ hours.

To make the baked beans, heat the butter and oil in a large saucepan, then add the lardons and cook until crispy. Add the paprika and cook for 2–3 minutes, stirring occasionally. Then stir in the sugar, bring to the boil and add the mustard powder, beans and passata. Cook for a further 5–10 minutes, season and sprinkle in the parsley.

Cut a cross in the top of each potato, add the butter, then top with the beans and grated cheese.

LAMB HOT POT
\
SERVES 6

2kg diced lamb shoulder
1 tablespoon plain flour
2 tablespoons vegetable oil
3 large onions, sliced
6 lamb's kidneys, cleaned and chopped
500ml lamb stock
1 tablespoon Worcestershire sauce
a few sprigs of rosemary (optional)
1kg Maris Piper potatoes, sliced
25g butter
sea salt and freshly ground black
    pepper

The key to this dish is the simplicity of the ingredients: best-quality lamb, which as we all know comes from the UK, combined with potatoes and either stock or water. The addition of kidneys will increase the flavour substantially, but the most important thing for me is the onions – make sure you use plenty and cook them down well.

Dust the lamb in flour.

Heat the oil in a large flameproof casserole dish over a medium heat and fry the lamb, in batches, until browned all over. Season each batch as you cook it, and set aside on a plate once cooked, until all the lamb is done.

Add the onions to the same dish, season again and cook, stirring every now and then, for 5 minutes until starting to soften. Pop the lamb back into the dish and add the kidneys. Pour in the stock and add the Worcestershire sauce and sprigs of rosemary, if using. Season well and stir.

Cover the dish with a lid, bring to the boil, then turn the heat down and simmer very gently over a low heat for 2 hours until the lamb is tender. To check, pull a piece apart with two forks – it should shred easily.

Preheat the oven to 180°C (160°C fan)/350°F/gas 4.

Spread the sliced potatoes all around the edges of the dish. Dot with butter, then season and cook, uncovered, in the oven for 45 minutes.

LOADED POTATO SKINS
WITH TOMAHAWK STEAK

\

SERVES 4

4 large baking potatoes
1 tomahawk steak
100g pancetta lardons
knob of butter
1 bunch of spring onions, sliced
200g Cheddar, grated
2 corn-on-the-cobs
1 beef stock cube
knob of butter
sea salt and freshly ground black
    pepper

FOR THE BBQ SAUCE
1 shallot, diced
1 garlic clove, sliced
1 red chilli, diced
200g brown sugar
100ml tomato ketchup
50ml dark soy sauce
2 tablespoons chipotle paste
1 small bunch of parsley, chopped

FOR THE CHIPOTLE BUTTER
100g butter
1 tablespoon chopped parsley
1 tablespoon chipotle paste

I once went filming around America and this dish sums up a lot of what I ate – it's food, but bloody tasty food, amazing meat with great filled potato skins and I love the addition of chipotle butter! This butter works with chicken, pork or just potato skins on their own.

Preheat the oven to 180°C (160°C fan)/350°F/gas 4.

Prick the potatoes all over, place on a baking tray and bake for 1½ hours. Once cooked, cut them in half and scoop out the insides into a bowl. Pop the skins back onto the baking tray.

Meanwhile, to make the BBQ sauce, gently heat all the ingredients together in a small pan until bubbling. Combine all the ingredients for the chipotle butter.

Heat a BBQ until very hot and the coals are white. Season the steak, place on the BBQ and seal on both sides, then continue to cook for 10 minutes, turning. Remove from the BBQ and allow to rest for 15 minutes.

Heat a frying pan and fry the pancetta until crispy. Add to the potato insides with the butter and spring onions and mix well. Pile the mixture into the potato skins and top with the cheese. Bake in the oven for 5 minutes, then remove from the oven and drizzle with half the BBQ sauce.

Place the corn on the BBQ and cook for 3–4 minutes, turning, until lightly charred.

To serve, crumble the stock cube over the steak and dot with some chipotle butter. Brush the remaining chipotle butter over the cooked corn-on-the-cobs. Pop the potatoes onto a platter, spoon over the remaining BBQ sauce and serve with the steak and corn-on-cobs on the side.

JACKET POTATOES WITH SLOPPY JOE SAUCE

\

SERVES 4

4 baking potatoes
8 pork sausages
25ml olive oil

FOR THE SAUCE
400g minced pork
1 onion, diced
1 garlic clove, sliced
1 green chilli, diced
200g brown sugar
100ml tomato ketchup
50ml dark soy sauce
50ml white wine vinegar
2 tablespoons chipotle paste
½ small bunch of coriander, chopped
½ small bunch of mint, chopped

TO SERVE
100g butter
2 tablespoons crispy fried onions
½ small bunch of coriander, chopped
½ small bunch of mint, chopped

We used to make this sauce in the restaurant and use it for our dirty burgers. We would often make it for staff chow and the chefs seemed to love it, especially with crispy fried onions, coriander and mint. The great thing about the sauce is that it works well on so many different things, even hot dogs.

Preheat the oven to 200°C (180°C fan)/400°F/gas 6.

Prick the potatoes all over, pop on a baking tray and bake for 1¼ hours.

Drizzle the sausages with oil and fry them in a non-stick frying pan until golden. Transfer to a baking tray and cook in the oven for 10 minutes.

Meanwhile, to make the sauce, heat a non-stick frying pan and, when hot, add all the ingredients. Bring to the boil, then simmer for 10 minutes, stirring occasionally.

To serve, pop the potatoes onto plates, cut a cross in each and squeeze up the flesh. Add the butter, then pile the sausages on top. Spoon over the sauce, then sprinkle over some crispy fried onions and herbs.

LOADED MEXICAN POTATO SKINS

\

SERVES 4

4 large baking potatoes
100g pancetta lardons
2 corn-on-the-cobs, kernels removed
200g Cheddar, grated

FOR THE SAUCE
250ml tomato ketchup
100ml maple syrup
50ml dark soy sauce
100g soft brown sugar
1 red or green chilli, sliced

TO SERVE
guacamole
sour cream
salsa
1 large bunch of coriander, chopped
2 red chillies, sliced

No book on potatoes would be complete without a combination of the ingredients below. This is another one of my favourite-tasting recipes – tons of flavour and a full-on meal, for very little money.

Preheat the oven to 180°C (160°C fan)/350°F/gas 4.

Prick the potatoes all over, place on a baking tray and bake for 1½ hours. Once cooked, cut them in half and scoop out the insides into a bowl. Pop the skins back onto the baking tray.

In a frying pan, fry the pancetta until it is crispy, then add the corn and cook, stirring, for 3–4 minutes until charred. Add the pancetta and corn to the potato insides and mix well. Pile the mixture into the potato skins and top each with the cheese. Bake in the oven for 5 minutes.

To make the sauce, heat all the ingredients gently in a small pan until the sugar has dissolved.

Pop the potatoes onto a platter, drizzle over the sauce and serve with guacamole, sour cream and salsa. Sprinkle over the coriander and chillies to complete the dish.

POTATO AND 'NDUJA PIZZAS

\

MAKES 10

FOR THE PIZZA DOUGH
1kg strong plain bread flour
20g fresh or dried yeast
50g semolina flour, plus extra
   for dusting
100ml olive oil
20g salt
650ml water

FOR THE TOPPING
400g can San Marzano tomatoes,
   blitzed until smooth
100g mini mozzarella balls
50g Pecorino, grated
400g cooked sliced potatoes
200g 'nduja
olive oil, for drizzling
a few sprigs of basil

Anybody who knows me, or who watches me on TV, knows that I love pizza. I am lucky to have a wood-fired pizza oven in the garden, and this is one of only a few different types of pizza that I enjoy, other than the classic Margherita. For me, the buck stops well before the word 'pineapple'...

Place all the ingredients for the dough into a stand mixer fitted with a dough hook attachment. Mix on a slow speed for 4 minutes, then turn up to a medium speed for 12 minutes.

Tip the dough onto a surface dusted with semolina flour and shape into 10 even-sized balls. Leave to prove for 15 minutes or cover and pop in the fridge overnight.

When you are ready to cook, heat a pizza oven until hot or alternatively place a pizza stone into an oven at 200°C (180°C fan)/400°F/gas 6 for 30 minutes.

Dust a work surface with semolina flour and roll a ball of the dough out as thin as you dare. Top with a smear of puréed tomato, some of the cheeses, potatoes and 'nduja. Drizzle over some olive oil, then place into the pizza oven or onto the pizza stone. Bake until crisp and bubbling in the centre. Repeat to make the remaining pizzas. Top the pizzas with some sprigs of basil to serve.

LOVAGE-CRUSTED FISH WITH SLICED POTATOES AND ASPARAGUS

\

SERVES 4

25ml olive oil
150g butter
4 x 200g brill fillets, skinned
300g new potatoes, sliced
12 asparagus spears, sliced
a few chives, chopped
sea salt and freshly ground black
    pepper
lemon wedges, to serve

FOR THE CRUST
30g lovage
50g Parmesan
1 thick slice of bread
1 small bunch of parsley
3 borage leaves
50g full-fat cream cheese

This recipe came about due to the massive lovage plant I had in the garden. We first used it to make a crust for lamb, then by adding a bit of cream cheese we turned it into a great crust for fish. We use plaice or brill in the restaurant, but it's good with any non-oily fish, although salmon works too. Lovage is a fascinating herb, which has got a sort of celery taste and smell and works brilliantly in a lot of dishes with potatoes – even soup.

To make the crust, place all the ingredients in a food processor and blitz until smooth. Put between 2 layers of greaseproof paper and, using a rolling pin, roll out to 3mm thick. Chill in the fridge until needed.

Preheat the oven to 200°C (180°C fan)/400°F/gas 6.

Heat a non-stick ovenproof pan, add the oil and 50g of the butter, then put in the fish. Season, then cook for 2 minutes. Flip over and cook for another 2 minutes.

Cut 4 pieces of crust to the same size as each piece of fish and sit on top of the fish. Place the pan in the oven and roast the fish for 5 minutes. Put the pan back on the hob, add 25g of the butter and cook for another minute.

Meanwhile, in a separate pan, cover the potato slices in water and the remaining 75g butter and cook for 10 minutes, adding the asparagus for the last 2 minutes of cooking time. Sprinkle with chives and season.

To serve, spoon the potato and asparagus onto plates and place the fish alongside with a lemon wedge for squeezing.

ROAST CHICKEN, BREAD SAUCE AND GAME CHIPS

\
SERVES 6

1.5kg whole chicken
a few sprigs of thyme
sea salt and freshly ground black
   pepper

FOR THE SAUCE
300ml veal stock
100ml white wine

FOR THE BREAD SAUCE
200ml full-fat milk
200ml double cream
1 onion studded with 5 cloves
1 bay leaf
150g fresh white breadcrumbs

FOR THE GAME CHIPS
vegetable oil, for deep-frying
2 large potatoes, peeled

Not many people know that a classic accompaniment to roast chicken is bread sauce and game chips, as it is for most roast game birds. You do need a proper mandoline though: as you slice the potato you turn it 90 degrees before slicing it again, which gives the chips their unique appearance. But whatever you do, watch your hands! And don't think you can use salt and vinegar crisps either!

Preheat the oven to 200°C (180°C fan)/400°F/gas 6.

Season the chicken, place into a roasting tray, sitting on the thyme sprigs. Pop into the oven and roast for 1½ hours. Remove the chicken from the roasting tray, place on a serving platter and set aside to rest.

Place the roasting tray over a medium heat, whisk in the stock and wine and leave to simmer until reduced by half.

Meanwhile, to make the bread sauce, place the milk, cream, clove-studded onion and bay leaf in a pan over a gentle heat and warm through. Remove and discard the onion and bay leaf. Add the breadcrumbs, stir in and keep warm.

To make the game chips, heat the oil in a deep-fat fryer or large pan to 170°C (340°F).

Slice the potatoes on the game-chip setting of a mandoline or slice very thinly. Deep-fry the chips until crisp and golden brown, drain onto kitchen paper and sprinkle with salt.

Pour the sauce over the chicken and serve with the bread sauce and game chips alongside.

MUSSELS WITH
POTATO FLATBREADS
\
SERVES 4

50g butter
1 onion, diced
2 celery sticks, diced
2 garlic cloves, crushed to a paste
250ml white wine
250ml double cream
2kg mussels, cleaned
1 small bunch of parsley, chopped
freshly ground black pepper

FOR THE FLATBREADS
300g self-raising flour, plus extra
    for dusting
100g thick Greek yogurt
100g potatoes, cooked and diced
pinch of salt, plus extra for scattering

Whenever I am in a restaurant I will choose a dish like this, as I absolutely adore simple mussels cooked in this style. We have it on the menu in the restaurant and it is one of the most popular starters or mains. We get our mussels from grade A waters in the River Exe, in Devon. I find that it has the best mussels around, so much so, we even sell them in the online shop to help the guy who produces them sell them direct to you.

Preheat the oven to 220°C (200°C fan)/425°F/gas 7.

To make the flatbreads, in a large bowl, mix the flour, yogurt, potatoes, salt and enough water to bring the dough together. Dust a work surface with flour and divide the dough in half. Roll out each piece into an oval about 1cm thick. Transfer onto a large baking tray dusted with flour and scatter each flatbread with salt. Bake in the oven for 8–10 minutes.

Heat a large casserole dish until hot, then add half the butter. When sizzling, add the onion, celery and garlic and sweat for a few minutes. Then add the wine, cream and some black pepper. Stir, then add the remaining butter. Pop the mussels in and give everything a big stir before popping on a lid. Cook for 4 minutes. Remove the lid and discard any mussels that haven't opened, then sprinkle over some chopped parsley.

Serve the flatbreads alongside the mussels.

PAN-ROAST DOVER SOLE WITH CRAB, CRUSHED JERSEY ROYALS AND SAUCE GRENOBLE

\

SERVES 2

2 x 500g Dover sole, skinned and
   filleted into 8 pieces
1 tablespoon vegetable oil
250g Jersey Royals
250g fresh white crab meat, picked
juice of 1 lemon
6 asparagus spears
1 punnet of baby pea shoots
1 punnet of baby basil
handful of croutons
sea salt and freshly ground black
   pepper

Credit where credit's due, Mark Jordan is a good mate of mine, and an amazing chef, and I had this dish at his restaurant, Mark Jordan at the Beach, in Jersey. Great cooks manage to make simple ingredients taste amazing and this dish just highlights that fact.

Preheat the oven to 180°C (160°C fan)/350°F/gas 4.

Place all the fillets of sole on top of each other, with the first fillet facing one way then the next facing the opposite way, like building a sole wall – so you have an 8-fillet-high wall.

Skewer the sole fillets together with 6 cocktail sticks and trim off the ends, then cut the stacked fillets neatly in half.

Heat a non-stick frying pan until hot and add the vegetable oil. Place the sole fillets in the pan and colour on one side until golden brown. Then flip over, place on a baking tray and cook in the oven for 4 minutes.

Meanwhile, place the potatoes in a saucepan of boiling salted water and boil for about 12 minutes until cooked, depending on size.

Drain and return to the pan. Crush the potatoes lightly using a fork, then add the crab meat and a squeeze of the lemon juice and mix well. Season to taste, then keep warm.

FOR THE SAUCE GRENOBLE
200g butter
110g caper berries
110g gherkins, finely diced
2 tablespoons chopped chives
juice of 2 lemons

To make the sauce, return the frying pan used to cook the fish to the heat, then add the butter and cook until nut brown. Add the caper berries and gherkins and heat through. Stir through the chopped chives and the lemon juice.

Bring a pan of salted water to the boil, drop the asparagus in and boil for 10 seconds, then drain.

Remove the sole from the oven and gently twist out the cocktail sticks, then squeeze over the remaining lemon juice.

To serve, place a spoonful of the potato mixture into a metal ring in the centre of each plate and top with a stack of Dover sole. Spoon the sauce Grenoble over and around the fish, then scatter the pea shoots, baby basil and croutons around the plate. Top each sole with 3 asparagus spears and serve straight away.

POTATO SAUSAGE TRAYBAKE

\

SERVES 4

8 pork sausages
600g Anya potatoes
2 red onions, cut into eighths
a few sprigs of thyme
a few sprigs of rosemary
a few sage leaves
100ml olive oil
sea salt and freshly ground black
    pepper

FOR THE ONION GRAVY
25g butter
1 onion, sliced
100ml Madeira
25ml sherry
500ml beef stock

I was brought up on this type of food – sausage and mash and simple traybakes. I have used Anya potatoes here, but if you can find them, this dish works equally well with Ratte potatoes. You have just got to be careful about their size; if they are too big, cut them in half.

Preheat the oven to 200°C (180°C fan)/400°F/gas 6.

Place the sausages, potatoes, red onions and herbs in a large roasting tray. Drizzle over the oil, season, then roast for 40 minutes.

For the gravy, heat a pan over a medium heat, add the butter and onion and cook for 10 minutes until the onion is deeply coloured. Add the Madeira, sherry and stock, bring to the boil and reduce by half. Season.

Serve the gravy alongside the potato sausage traybake.

RED MULLET WITH VEGETABLES À LA GRECQUE AND ROUILLE

\

SERVES 2

500g red mullet, filleted
sea salt and freshly ground black
  pepper

FOR THE ROUILLE
3 egg yolks
75ml extra virgin olive oil
3 garlic cloves, crushed
1 baked potato (about 150g), insides
  scooped out while still warm
good pinch of saffron threads
pinch of cayenne pepper

FOR THE VEGETABLES
À LA GRECQUE
50ml white wine vinegar
125ml olive oil
25g tomato purée
50ml lemon juice
1 garlic clove, crushed
1 sprig of thyme
1 bay leaf
1 sprig of rosemary
½ teaspoon coriander seeds, crushed
½ teaspoon black peppercorns,
  crushed
25g sugar
1 teaspoon sea salt
2 baby fennel, quartered
4 runner beans, sliced
8 baby onions, peeled
4 baby carrots
2 baby courgettes, halved

My advice to any keen cook is that you need to learn how to make a mayonnaise and, once you have mastered that, a good rouille. This classic accompaniment is usually found in bouillabaisse, the fish stew from Marseille. But it works brilliantly with fish like red mullet and salmon, so give it a go! Just be careful not to use too much saffron though.

To make the rouille, place the egg yolks in a mini blender and, with the machine running, add the oil slowly. Then add the garlic, potato, saffron, cayenne and a pinch of salt and blitz until smooth. Pop into a bowl and set aside.

Preheat the grill to medium.

Season the mullet, then grill the fish for 4–5 minutes.

For the vegetables, bring the vinegar, olive oil, tomato purée, lemon juice, garlic, herbs, coriander seeds, peppercorns, sugar, salt and 75ml water to the boil in a large pan. Add the prepared vegetables. Cook for 4–5 minutes until just tender, then drain and serve with the fish, some of the cooking liquor and the rouille.

MAXIM RAGOUT WITH BEEF CHEEKS

\
SERVES 4

2kg beef cheeks
2 tablespoons plain flour
2 tablespoons olive oil
150g pancetta, cut into small chunks
1 shallot, finely chopped
2 onions, sliced
1 garlic clove, crushed
75ml brandy
500ml Burgundy red wine
250ml beef stock
1 bouquet garni (2 bay leaves, 2 sprigs
    of thyme, 2 sprigs of flat-leaf parsley)
125g butter
110g small baby onions
200g chestnut mushrooms
1kg floury potatoes, peeled and thinly
    sliced
sea salt and freshly ground black
    pepper

This is a dish that we made at an old restaurant of mine, and it was one that food critic Jay Rayner raved about, and which I have subsequently cooked for him on TV. Beef cheeks have an amazing texture due to their size, as the meat stays beautifully moist and tender because you can keep the pieces as a portion, rather than diced, like stewing meat.

Toss the beef with the flour and some salt and black pepper.

Heat a flameproof casserole dish until hot, add half the olive oil and the pancetta and fry for 1–2 minutes until golden brown. Add the beef and fry until browned on each side. Add the shallot, onions and garlic and fry until just softened.

Add the brandy and turn up the heat to burn off the alcohol. Pour in the red wine and beef stock and bring to a simmer. Add the bouquet garni, then cover and cook over a low heat for 2 hours until tender and the sauce has just thickened.

Heat a frying pan until hot, add 25g of the butter and the remaining oil and fry the baby onions until just golden.

Add to the casserole along with the chestnut mushrooms and cook for a further 20 minutes until tender.

Preheat the oven to 200°C (180°C fan)/400°F/gas 6.

Lay the sliced potatoes all around the edges of the casserole, buttering liberally with the remaining butter, then pop in the oven for 25–30 minutes until golden and crisp.

RIBS WITH CIDER SAUCE AND JACKET POTATOES

\

SERVES 6

FOR THE RIBS
2kg pork ribs
1 onion
2 carrots
1 bulb of garlic
1 small bunch of parsley
a few black peppercorns
10 star anise
1 tablespoon fennel seeds
2 cinnamon sticks

FOR THE SAUCE
100g butter
100g caster sugar
100ml treacle
100ml condensed milk
75ml cider

FOR THE POTATOES
6 large baking potatoes
olive oil, for coating
1 tablespoon sea salt
200g butter

One of the best-tasting BBQ-style sauces I have had in a long time, this comes from the fabulous Sam Head, who has been working with me for nigh-on three decades. She lived in America for a few years and brought this recipe back with her... delicious!

Put the ribs and remaining rib ingredients in large pan. Add just enough water to cover, bring to the boil and simmer for 45 minutes. Remove the ribs from the pan.

To make the sauce, put all the ingredients in a pan and bring to the boil. Remove from the heat and set aside until needed.

Heat a BBQ until the coals are grey, place the ribs onto the BBQ and cook for 15–20 minutes until coloured. Brush the sauce all over the ribs and cook for a further 3–4 minutes.

Meanwhile, preheat the oven to 200°C (180°C fan)/400°F/gas 6.

To make the jacket potatoes, prick the potatoes all over and place on a baking tray. Coat in olive oil, sprinkle with sea salt and bake for 1–1½ hours.

Remove from the oven, split and fill each potato with the butter. Serve alongside the ribs.

WHISKY AND ORANGE MUSTARD RIB OF BEEF WITH POTATO AND TURNIP DAUPHINOISE

\

SERVES 6

4kg 3-bone forerib of 28-day aged beef
vegetable oil, for frying
200ml white wine
300ml beef stock

FOR THE MUSTARD
150ml cider vinegar
5 tablespoons caster sugar
60g yellow mustard seeds
25g brown mustard seeds
2 tablespoons English mustard powder
50ml single malt whisky
50ml orange juice
sea salt and freshly ground black
 pepper

This dauphinoise works really well with the combination of white turnips and potatoes. The idea is to thinly slice both vegetables, so they randomly mix through the dish. It's also brilliant when cold, as you can slice it into 2.5cm-thick slices and pan-fry them.

To make the mustard, place the vinegar and sugar in a saucepan and bring to a simmer. Add both mustard seeds and powder and stir well. Simmer over a high heat for 3 minutes until the liquid has reduced by half and the seeds are slightly softened.

Pour into a food blender and blitz to a purée – it takes a good couple of minutes, then the seeds will break down and the mustard becomes creamy. Add the whisky and orange juice and blitz once more. Season with a little salt and black pepper. Use immediately or spoon into jars and seal.

Preheat the oven to 200°C (180°C fan)/400°F/gas 6.

Spread some of the mustard all over the beef. Heat a large frying pan until very hot, then add a little oil to the pan and fry the beef on all sides until nicely browned. Transfer to a roasting tray and place in the oven for 1½ hours.

Remove the beef from the oven, cover with foil and rest for 15–30 minutes.

FOR THE DAUPHINOISE POTATOES

50g butter
1 garlic clove, halved
500g King Edward potatoes, peeled and thinly sliced
500g turnips, peeled and thinly sliced
300ml double cream
300ml full-fat milk
pinch of freshly grated nutmeg

Place the beef on a board to carve, then place the roasting tray over a medium heat until bubbling, add the wine and cook until reduced by half. Add the beef stock and cook until reduced by half again, then season to taste.

Meanwhile, butter an ovenproof dish with a little of the butter, then rub the garlic clove around the dish.

Add the sliced potatoes and turnips to a bowl. Toss together, season with salt and black pepper, then tip into the dish, pressing the slices down so you end up with an even layer.

Place the cream and milk in a bowl and whisk to combine. Season with salt, black pepper and nutmeg and pour over the potatoes and turnips. Dot with the remaining butter and cover tightly with foil. Cook in the oven for 1 hour until the vegetables are just tender. After 1 hour, carefully remove the foil and return to the oven for a further 30 minutes until golden brown on top.

To serve, carve the beef and serve with a spoonful of dauphinoise and dollop of mustard. Drizzle over the pan juices to finish.

POMMES PARISIENNE WITH PORK CHOPS AND CHESTNUTS

\

SERVES 6

6 thick-cut pork chops
sea salt and freshly ground black
    pepper

FOR THE POMMES PARISIENNE
500g potatoes, peeled and scooped out
    with a melon baller
knob of butter
6 sprigs of thyme, 2 leaves picked,
    4 left whole
500ml veal jus
4 garlic cloves, chopped
1 shallot, finely sliced
100g chestnuts, chopped

When I knew I was writing a book on potatoes, this was one of the dishes that brought back so many memories of being a student at college and the years of training in my teens, as it used to be a very, very famous potato dish, and to my mind, it still should be. I remember using a Parisienne scoop, otherwise known as a melon baller, to get the shape. The idea is that the potatoes cook in the stock, and as it reduces you get this amazing glaze to roll them around in at the end.

To make the pommes Parisienne, place the potato balls in a large frying pan and sprinkle with a splash of cold water and the butter. Sprinkle over the thyme leaves.

Add half of the veal jus to the potatoes and simmer.

In a separate pan, add the remaining jus, the garlic, shallot and the thyme sprigs. Cook until the jus has reduced by half. Pour over the potatoes to create a glaze. Sprinkle over the chopped chestnuts.

Meanwhile, preheat the grill to high.

Place the pork chops on a baking tray and season. Cook under the grill for 6 minutes, turn and grill for a further 6 minutes.

Serve the potatoes as a garnish to the pork and drizzle with any remaining glaze from the pan.

CHEESY POTATO BRIOCHE LEEKS

\

SERVES 6

100g butter
200ml double cream
a few sprigs of thyme, leaves picked
600g cooked new potatoes
600g leeks, sliced
250g Cheddar, grated
200g fresh brioche, cubed
sea salt and freshly ground black
   pepper

We cook this in the restaurants when the temperature changes from summer to autumn. It sells so well; the brioche adds to the flavour, and you can use any cooked potatoes that you like. The key is to thinly slice the leeks, so they don't cook for too long, and season them well.

Preheat the oven to 200°C (180°C fan)/400°F/gas 6.

Add the butter, cream and thyme to a large pan over a medium heat. Add the potatoes and leeks and cook for 2–3 minutes until soft. Stir in half the cheese.

Place the brioche cubes in an ovenproof dish and toast in the oven for 2–3 minutes until golden and crisp. Top with the potato and leek mixture, scatter over the remaining cheese, season and bake for a further 10 minutes.

T-BONE STEAK WITH BORDELAISE SAUCE AND POTATOES PARISIENNE WITH WILD MUSHROOMS

\
SERVES 2

25ml olive oil
2 T-bone steaks
½ bulb of garlic
a few sprigs of thyme
25g butter
sea salt and freshly ground black
    pepper

FOR THE SAUCE
75g butter
3 shallots, diced
1 bulb of garlic, halved
200ml red wine
500ml beef stock

FOR THE POTATOES
300ml beef stock
2 large potatoes, peeled and scooped
    out with a melon baller
100g wild mushrooms
25g butter

This is certainly one of the most popular sauces we serve in the restaurant in Manchester, which just goes to prove that classics will always stand the test of time.

Preheat the oven to 200°C (180°C fan)/400°F/gas 6.

Heat an ovenproof frying pan, then add the oil, followed by the steaks, garlic and thyme. Pan-fry the steaks for 2 minutes on each side, then season. Pop the frying pan into the oven for 15 minutes. Remove from the oven, add the butter to the hot pan and spoon the melted butter over the steaks. Set aside to rest.

To make the sauce, melt the butter in a separate frying pan, add the shallots and garlic and fry for 2–3 minutes. Pour in the wine and stock and allow to simmer until reduced by half. Keep warm.

For the potatoes, add the stock and potatoes to a separate frying pan over a medium heat and cook for about 15 minutes until the stock has completely evaporated and the potatoes are sticky. Add the mushrooms and butter for the last couple of minutes of cooking time. Season.

To serve, place the steaks on plates with the potatoes and mushrooms alongside and pour over the sauce.

SAUSAGES WITH GUINNESS-BRAISED ONIONS AND MASH

\

SERVES 4

4 onions, peeled and halved
25g butter
400ml Guinness
200ml beef stock
25ml vegetable oil
12 pork sausages
sea salt and freshly ground black
    pepper

FOR THE MASH
100g butter
100ml double cream
1kg Maris Piper potatoes, peeled,
    boiled and put through a ricer
sea salt and white pepper

Having just come back from a golf trip to Ireland with Mr Brian Turner, John Williams and Galton Blackiston, I now realise what makes a good pint of Guinness, and to be fair, Galton realised it too much! The last thing he would have wanted the day after was this dish put in front of him. Shame, as it tastes bloody amazing.

Place the onion halves cut-side down in a large frying pan with the butter and cook until deeply coloured. Pour in the Guinness and stock, bring to the boil and then reduce the heat and simmer for 30 minutes.

Heat a frying pan, add the oil, then the sausages and pan-fry until deeply coloured.

For the mash, add the butter and cream to the mashed potato and mix thoroughly. Season with salt and white pepper.

Serve a big spoonful of the mash with the sausages and onion gravy.

CLASSIC SAUSAGES WITH GRAVY AND MASH

\

SERVES 4

25ml lard or Iberico pork fat
12 pork sausages

FOR THE ONION GRAVY
1 tablespoon lard
2 onions, sliced
25ml Madeira
200ml chicken stock
200ml veal stock
1 teaspoon Marmite
1 teaspoon Bovril
knob of butter
sea salt and freshly ground black
    pepper

FOR THE MASH
100g butter
1kg Maris Piper potatoes, peeled,
    boiled and put through a ricer
100ml double cream
sea salt and white pepper

If you're not into Guinness and want simple, great-tasting gravy, then this is the one, I promise you. It's my mum's old secret recipe made with Bovril and Marmite, and it's a winner every time.

To make the gravy, heat a pan over a medium heat, add the lard and onions and cook for 10 minutes until the onions are deeply coloured. Add the Madeira, both stocks, the Marmite and Bovril and bring to the boil, then simmer for 5 minutes. Season, then stir in the butter.

Meanwhile, heat a frying pan, add the lard or Iberico fat, then the sausages and pan-fry until deeply coloured.

For the mash, melt the butter in a saucepan, add the mashed potato and cream and mix thoroughly. Season with salt and white pepper.

Serve a big spoonful of the mash with the sausages and gravy.

POTATO AND SPINACH CURRY

\

SERVES 4

1 tablespoon vegetable oil
1 onion, diced
4cm piece of fresh ginger, minced
2 garlic cloves, chopped
1 teaspoon mild chilli powder
2 teaspoons garam masala
1 green chilli, halved lengthways
400g can chopped tomatoes
2 fresh tomatoes, chopped
400g new potatoes
50ml double cream
50g butter
200g baby spinach

For me, most curries don't need meat, as vegetables should take the limelight, and this dish is one of many that proves it. You can use any potatoes you wish, just make sure that you cut them down in size if they are large, so that they cook evenly.

Heat a large pan, add the oil and onion and fry for 10 minutes. Then add the ginger, garlic, chilli powder, garam masala, chilli, canned and fresh tomatoes and potatoes. Stir through and simmer for 15 minutes.

Add the cream, butter and spinach and stir until the spinach is just wilted, then serve.

SIRLOIN STEAK WITH CHIPS AND BÉARNAISE SAUCE

\

SERVES 2

2 x 150g sirloin steaks
25g butter
sea salt and freshly ground black
  pepper

FOR THE BÉARNAISE SAUCE
1 shallot, finely diced
1 small bunch of tarragon, chopped
50ml white wine vinegar
4 egg yolks
300g clarified butter
juice of 1 lemon

TO SERVE
chips (page 187)
a few sprigs of watercress

The best dish ever invented! Whether you are using French fries or frozen chips, it's one of my favourites.

Heat a non-stick frying pan over a high heat and season the steaks. Melt the butter in the pan and, when foaming, add the steaks and cook for 2 minutes, then flip over and cook for 1 minute. Rest the steaks on a warm plate.

In a separate pan, add the shallot, half the tarragon and the vinegar. Bring to the boil, then remove from the heat and strain the vinegar into a jug, discarding the shallot and tarragon.

In a bowl over a pan of simmering water, whisk the egg yolks with the infused vinegar and slowly add the clarified butter, whisking continuously. Stir in the remaining tarragon and lemon juice.

Serve the steaks with the watercress, béarnaise sauce and chips on the side.

POTATO, CHICKEN AND
BACON CAESAR SALAD
\
SERVES 6

3 thick-cut slices of white bread
1 large chicken, spatchcocked and
   slashed
1 small bunch of thyme
1 small bunch of rosemary
12 slices of bacon
50ml olive oil
1 lemon, halved
sea salt and freshly ground black
   pepper

FOR THE DRESSING
2 egg yolks
1 tablespoon Dijon mustard
4 garlic cloves, poached in wine or
   water for 3 minutes and drained
2 anchovies
200ml vegetable oil
1 tablespoon white wine vinegar
50g Parmesan, grated

TO SERVE
600g new potatoes, cooked
selection of winter salad leaves

One of the many ideas my chefs came up with, this salad is Adam Summers' recipe and not only does it taste great, but it also looks spectacular.

Preheat the oven to 220°C (200°C fan)/425°F/gas 7.

Place the bread in a roasting tray, top with the chicken, herbs and bacon. Season and drizzle over the oil. Pop the lemon halves around the chicken, place in the oven and roast for 45 minutes. Set aside to rest for 15 minutes.

To make the dressing, blitz the egg yolks and mustard in a food processor, then add the garlic and anchovies. Slowly drizzle in the oil until thick, then add the vinegar and Parmesan. If you prefer a thinner dressing, add a splash of water.

Chop the toasted bread into croutons. Cut the chicken and bacon into bite-sized pieces. Place in a large bowl and add the potatoes and salad leaves. Drizzle over the dressing and garnish with the roasted lemon halves.

WEEPING STUFFED LEG OF LAMB WITH ROAST POTATOES, CARROTS, CABBAGE, MINT SAUCE AND GRAVY

\

SERVES 6-8

1 boned leg of lamb
zest and juice of 2 lemons
1 small bunch of rosemary, chopped
100g breadcrumbs
100g almonds, chopped
2 eggs

FOR THE POTATOES
1kg Maris Piper potatoes, peeled
    and halved if large
300g goose fat

FOR THE CARROTS
500g large carrots
50g butter
25g caster sugar
4 star anise

FOR THE SPRING CABBAGE
400g cabbage, shredded
50g butter

FOR THE MINT SAUCE
1 large bunch of mint, chopped
50g caster sugar
100ml malt vinegar
pinch of salt

TO SERVE
lamb gravy

Apologies for the title, but the idea of this dish is to cook the lamb on the oven rack so that its cooking juices and fats drip on to the roasted vegetables below, including the potatoes. This method also works well with chicken, beef and pork.

Preheat the oven to 200°C (180°C fan)/400°F/gas 6.

Unroll the lamb. In a small bowl, mix together the lemon zest and juice, rosemary, breadcrumbs, almonds and eggs. Spread the mixture all over the inside of the lamb, then season and roll up. Tie up with kitchen string, pop onto a baking tray on a rack and roast in the oven for 2 hours.

Meanwhile, pop the potatoes into a pan of cold salted water and bring to the boil. Put the goose fat into a roasting tin and place in the oven. Cook the potatoes for 15 minutes, then drain and add to the roasting tin for the last 45 minutes of cooking the lamb.

For the carrots, put the carrots into a separate pan, cover with water and add all the remaining ingredients. Bring to the boil and cook for 20 minutes, then drain.

For the cabbage, put it in a separate pan with the butter and 100ml water over a medium heat, and cook for 2 minutes.

To make the mint sauce, put all the ingredients in a pan and warm through gently for a minute, then pour into a small bowl.

To serve, warm the gravy and serve with the lamb and vegetables, with the mint sauce on the side.

SALAD NIÇOISE WITH TUNA

\

SERVES 4-6

6 eggs
2 little butterhead lettuces, leaves
    separated
1 red chicory, leaves separated
200g green beans, blanched
50g stoned black olives
6 anchovies
100g Jersey Royals, cooked and halved
    if large
100g cherry tomatoes, halved

FOR THE FISH
25ml olive oil
4 x 200g portions of tuna
sea salt and freshly ground black
    pepper

FOR THE DRESSING
1 tablespoon water
1 tablespoon Dijon mustard
150ml vegetable oil
50ml white wine vinegar
juice of 1 lemon
1 garlic clove, minced with a pinch
    of salt

This classic dish from the south of France is a true winner, as we all know, but interestingly there are many different variations wherever you go, even in France. However, the potatoes, black olives and green beans seem to feature in all of them.

Bring a large saucepan of water to a rolling boil, add the eggs and boil for 6 minutes. Plunge the eggs into cold water and remove the shells, taking care to not break the eggs.

For the fish, heat a non-stick frying pan until hot. Drizzle the oil over both sides of the tuna and season. Add to the pan and cook for 1 minute, then flip over and cook for another minute. Remove from the pan and slice.

For the dressing, put all the ingredients into a large bowl and whisk together, then season.

To serve, arrange all the leaves on a platter and top with the green beans, olives, anchovies, potatoes and tomatoes. Cut the eggs cleanly in half and nestle into the salad. To finish, dot the tuna around and spoon over the dressing.

SLOW-ROAST SHOULDER OF PORK WITH APPLE SAUCE

\

SERVES 6–8

3.5kg boned shoulder of pork
olive oil, for rubbing
sea salt and freshly ground black
 pepper

FOR THE APPLE SAUCE
2 Bramley apples, peeled, cored
 and grated
50g butter
75ml cider
2–4 tablespoons caster sugar, to taste

TO SERVE
1kg mashed potato
100g butter
100ml double cream
300ml veal jus

Whenever I am filming, this seems to be the most popular dish without a doubt, not only with the crew and guests, but also with people watching and searching online for the recipe. The key to proper crackling is to shock the pork first and then reduce the oven temperature, it never seems to work the other way round.

Preheat the oven to 240°C (220°C fan)/475°F/gas 9.

Score the skin of the pork into diamonds with a sharp knife and rub the surface with olive oil and sea salt.

Place in a deep-sided roasting tray, pour in 600ml water and transfer to the oven, uncovered, for 40 minutes. Then cover with foil and reduce the oven temperature to 150°C (130°C fan)/300°F/gas 2 and cook for 3½ hours until very tender and golden brown. Remove from the oven and rest for 30 minutes.

To make the sauce, place the apples, butter and cider into a saucepan, cover and place over a medium heat. Cook for about 4–5 minutes until the apples have broken down. Stir, then season with the sugar and a little salt.

Heat the mashed potato in a saucepan with the butter and cream and mix thoroughly.

Add the veal jus to a separate saucepan over a medium heat and cook until reduced by half, then season.

Slice the pork and serve with the apple sauce, mashed potato and reduced jus.

SPANISH CHICKEN, PARMENTIER POTATOES AND GREEN BEANS

\
SERVES 4

1 red pepper, cored and chopped
1 yellow pepper, cored and chopped
1 bulb of garlic
400g can chopped tomatoes
400g fresh tomatoes
1 small bunch of fresh thyme
1 large chicken, spatchcocked
140ml olive oil
400g green beans
2 shallots, diced
200g chorizo sausage, sliced
juice of 2 lemons
2 tablespoons smoked paprika
sea salt and freshly ground black
    pepper

FOR THE PARMENTIER POTATOES
4 large potatoes, diced
100ml olive oil
1 bulb of garlic, crushed
a few sprigs of rosemary

José Pizarro is a great mate of mine and one who I learn a lot about Spanish food from, although I have been a fan of this cuisine for years. The addition of chorizo to chicken and potatoes, with plenty of olive oil, proves Spain has so much to offer in the way of food – they really do produce some amazing ingredients.

Preheat the oven to 200°C (180°C fan)/400°F/gas 6.

Cover the base of a large roasting tray with the peppers, garlic and tomatoes, then sprinkle over the thyme. Pop the chicken on top, drizzle over 25ml of the olive oil, and roast in the oven for 1½ hours.

Meanwhile, toss the potatoes in the oil, garlic and rosemary in a bowl, then season. Place in a single layer in a roasting tray and roast for 25 minutes until golden and crisp.

Cook the beans in boiling salted water for 3 minutes, then drain. Heat a frying pan over medium heat, add 1 tablespoon of olive oil and pan-fry the drained beans, shallots and chorizo for 2 minutes.

Mix the remaining 100ml olive oil, the lemon juice and paprika in a small jug and season. Spoon over the chicken just before serving with the potatoes and green beans.

THAI GREEN CURRY
WITH SEA BASS
\
SERVES 2

400ml can coconut milk
400g new potatoes, halved
200g baby spinach
1 whole sea bass, gutted and
   skin scored
sea salt and freshly ground black
   pepper

FOR THE PASTE
5cm piece of galangal, peeled
3 garlic cloves
2 green chillies
1 lemongrass stem, tough outer
   leaves removed
50ml vegetable oil, plus extra if needed
3 makrut lime leaves
1 small bunch of coriander, plus extra
   to serve
1 bunch of Thai basil
1 teaspoon caster sugar
1 tablespoon fish sauce

TO SERVE
fresh coconut shavings (optional)

Making your own Thai curry paste makes a massive difference to your final dish compared with using a ready-made version, mainly because of the fresh herbs. This curry works with any fish or even vegetables like aubergine and courgettes.

Place all the ingredients for the paste in a food processor and blitz to a rough paste. You may need to add a little extra vegetable oil.

Put the paste into a large pan over a medium heat and fry for 1 minute, then add the coconut milk. Stir through and simmer for 1 minute, then add the potatoes and simmer for 15 minutes. Add the spinach and stir through until wilted.

Meanwhile, heat the grill until hot. Place the fish onto a baking tray, season and grill for 10–12 minutes.

To serve, spoon the potato curry into the centre of a serving dish, spoon over the sauce and top with the fish. Sprinkle with extra coriander and fresh coconut shavings, if desired.

SPANISH FISH STEW WITH SAFFRON POTATOES

\

SERVES 6

100g chorizo sausage, diced
100ml white wine
1 litre passata
1 large jar of roasted red peppers,
    drained and chopped
25ml olive oil
4 garlic cloves, chopped
pinch of saffron threads
1 tablespoon smoked paprika
300g large prawns, shell on
6 scallops, cleaned
250g cockles, cleaned
250g mussels, cleaned
400g can haricot beans, washed
    and drained
1 tablespoon sherry vinegar
sea salt and freshly ground black
    pepper

FOR THE SAFFRON POTATOES
12 medium potatoes, peeled
pinch of saffron threads

Whenever I travel to Spain, this is one of the dishes that I always look out for on the menu. Chorizo and seafood is a great combination, and when served alongside simple saffron potatoes they taste even more amazing.

Pop the potatoes into a pan of boiling salted water, add the saffron and cook for 20 minutes until soft, then drain.

Meanwhile, heat a frying pan over a medium heat and pan-fry the chorizo until crispy. Add the wine and heat until bubbly, then add the passata, peppers, olive oil, garlic, saffron and paprika. Simmer for a few minutes.

Add all the seafood and the beans and season. Pop the lid on and cook for 5 minutes, then stir in the vinegar. Discard any clams or mussels that don't open.

To serve, put a portion of stew onto each plate with saffron potatoes alongside.

SPANISH TORTILLA

\

SERVES 2

5 eggs
25g butter
1 onion, diced
200g charred red peppers from a jar,
    sliced
300g potatoes, cooked and diced
sea salt and freshly ground black
    pepper

A great-tasting brunch dish that uses potatoes to bulk out the omelette along with vegetables, particularly wood-roasted or charred peppers from a jar, which seem a bit of a bargain considering the amount of flavour they provide.

Whisk together the eggs in a large bowl and season.

Heat a large non-stick pan over a high heat and add the butter. When the butter is foaming, add the onion and cook for 5 minutes until coloured, then add the egg mixture.

Turn the heat down to medium. Scatter the peppers and potatoes over the egg and cook for 10 minutes until the frittata is firm. Turn out onto a serving plate to serve.

ON THE SIDE

POMMES ALIGOT

\
SERVES 4

1kg Yukon Gold potatoes, peeled
   and diced
2 garlic cloves, minced
100g butter
100ml double cream
500g Tomme d'Auvergne or Tomme de
   l'Aubrac, or 250g mozzarella and
   250g Gruyère, rind removed and
   diced

This is the best cheesy mash you will ever have, just look
at it! It's a good idea to search for the right cheese, however,
as this will produce the right consistency, as will the Yukon
Gold potatoes.

Cook the potatoes in lots of boiling salted water until you can
pierce them easily. Drain.

Pass the cooked potatoes through a ricer. Return to the pan
and beat in the garlic, butter and cream, then half the cheese.
Beat until fully mixed, then add the rest of the cheese and
beat again before serving.

ALMOND DUCHESS POTATOES

\

SERVES 2

400g Marabel potatoes
pinch of nutmeg
3 egg yolks
25g butter, melted
25g flaked almonds
sea salt and freshly ground black
  pepper

This is proper classic cooking; simple baked potatoes passed through a ricer, with the addition of egg yolks and nutmeg, then piped into that traditional tower shape. I remember cooking these at college and they can often be found on the menu in the best French restaurants.

Preheat the oven to 180°C (160°C fan)/350°F/gas 4. Place the potatoes on a baking tray and bake for 1¼ hours. Scoop out the middles and pop through a ricer.

Increase the oven temperature to 200°C (180°C fan)/400°F/gas 6. Line a baking tray with baking parchment.

Warm the riced potatoes in a pan over a medium heat, then beat in the nutmeg, seasoning and egg yolks. Transfer to a piping bag, then pipe 4 swirls onto the prepared tray. Brush with the melted butter, sprinkle over the almonds and bake in the oven for 10 minutes until golden and hot. Great served with lamb chops.

HASSELBACK POTATOES

\

SERVES 4

800g new potatoes
75g butter, melted
25ml olive oil
a few sprigs of rosemary
sea salt and freshly ground black
    pepper

The idea of cutting potatoes like this is that you get a much crispier roasted new potato. The key, however, is cutting them down enough so that they open up during cooking but not so much that you cut them into pieces.

Preheat the oven to 200°C (180°C fan)/400°F/gas 6.

Place the potatoes between the handles of 2 wooden spoons and cut them at 2mm intervals until the knife hits the handles, so you don't slice them all the way through. Pop the potatoes onto a roasting tray. Drizzle over the butter and oil, sprinkle over the rosemary and season. Roast in the oven for 45 minutes–1 hour.

Serve with fish, lamb chops or chicken breast.

BOMBAY POTATOES

\

SERVES 6

2 tablespoons vegetable oil

1 onion, diced

5cm piece fresh ginger, grated

2 green chillies, halved lengthways

3 garlic cloves, sliced

1 tablespoon black mustard seeds

2 teaspoons ground coriander

1 teaspoon ground turmeric

1 teaspoon ground cumin

3 teaspoons garam masala

300ml passata

1kg new potatoes, cooked and halved
    if large

1 teaspoon sea salt

handful of fresh coriander, chopped,
    to serve

The great Cyrus Todiwala, who is an amazing Indian chef and a good mate of mine, taught me this dish and I have made it ever since. The most important thing to remember is not to burn the spices while cooking, as the most common mistake people make is to add dry spices to a dry pan, which means they can burn.

In a large non-stick pan, add the oil and the onion and fry for 10 minutes until deeply coloured. Pop in the ginger, chillies, garlic and spices and cook for another 5 minutes. Pour over the passata, bring to the boil, then blitz until smooth using a stick blender.

Pop the cooked potatoes into the tomato sauce and cook for 3–4 minutes until hot. Season with the salt, sprinkle over the coriander and serve alongside your favourite curry.

DAUPHINOISE POTATOES

\

SERVES 6-8

butter, for greasing
3 garlic cloves, chopped
10 Maris Piper potatoes, peeled and
    sliced thinly
100ml full-fat milk
100ml double cream
½ nutmeg, grated
75g Gruyère, grated
sea salt and freshly ground black
    pepper

I use Maris Pipers for a dauphinoise as I find they soak in the liquid and cook evenly without drying out. The most important thing is to use double cream and milk; some people use just milk, but cream makes the dish much richer.

Preheat the oven to 180°C (160°C fan)/350°F/gas 4.

Grease a 28cm round ovenproof dish with butter and rub the garlic all over the dish. Layer up the potatoes, cover in the milk and cream and season well. Sprinkle over the nutmeg and cheese and bake for 1 hour.

Serve with roast chicken or beef, or a rack of lamb.

DIRTY FRIES

\

SERVES 6

1kg frozen skinny fries
12 slices of streaky bacon
1 bunch of spring onions, sliced
2 red peppers, cored and sliced
2 tablespoons Cajun seasoning
400g Cheddar, grated

Just look at it – enjoy! A chef's guilty pleasure...

Heat a deep-fat fryer to 170°C (340°F). Preheat the oven to 200°C (180°C fan)/400°F/gas 6.

Fry the skinny fries for 8 minutes until golden and crisp, then drain on kitchen paper.

Meanwhile, fry the bacon until crisp, then add the spring onions and peppers and cook for 3–4 minutes, adding the Cajun seasoning for the final 2 minutes.

Spoon the fries onto a baking tray, scatter over the bacon and spicy vegetables, top with the cheese, then bake for 10 minutes until hot and bubbling.

DUCHESS POTATOES

\

SERVES 2

400g Marabel potatoes
pinch of nutmeg
3 egg yolks
2 tomatoes, peeled, deseeded and diced
a few sprigs of tarragon, chopped
½ shallot, diced
25g butter, melted
sea salt and freshly ground black pepper

Preheat the oven to 180°C (160°C fan)/350°F/gas 4.

Place the potatoes on a baking tray and bake for 1¼ hours. Scoop out the middles and pass through a ricer.

Increase the oven temperature to 200°C (180°C fan)/400°F/gas 6. Line a baking tray with baking parchment.

Warm the riced potato in a pan and beat in the nutmeg, egg yolks and seasoning. Transfer to a piping bag, then pipe 2 nests onto the prepared tray. Fill each nest with tomatoes, tarragon and shallot and brush with melted butter. Bake in the oven for 10 minutes until golden and hot.

Serve with chicken, duck or salmon.

FONDANT POTATOES

\

SERVES 6

6 medium Maris Piper potatoes, peeled
1 teaspoon vegetable oil
200g butter
4 large garlic cloves
a few sprigs of thyme
200ml chicken or beef stock
sea salt and freshly ground black pepper

Slice the ends off the potatoes so they lie flat, then cut into circles.

Heat a non-stick frying pan over a medium heat, add the oil, then the potatoes and cook them for 6 minutes until deep golden brown. Flip over and repeat on the other side. Add the butter and, when foaming, add the garlic, thyme and stock and cook, covered, for 25 minutes.

Serve with steak, beef stew or roast chicken.

POMMES ANNA

\
SERVES 4

100g melted butter, plus extra for greasing
4 Maris Piper potatoes, peeled and sliced thinly
sea salt and freshly ground black pepper

Preheat the oven to 180°C (160°C fan)/350°F/gas 4.

Grease a 20cm ovenproof dish with butter.
Layer up the potatoes, pouring over some
butter on each layer and seasoning as you go.
Bake for 1–1¼ hours.

Serve with roast pork or a leg of lamb.

POMMES PARISIENNE

\
SERVES 4

2 King Edward potatoes, peeled and flesh scooped
    out with a melon baller
1 garlic clove
a few sprigs of thyme, chopped
300ml beef stock
25g butter
sea salt and freshly ground black pepper

Add the potato balls to a saucepan with the garlic,
thyme and stock and cook over a medium heat
for 15 minutes until the stock has completely
evaporated and the potatoes are sticky. Finish with
butter, season and serve.

SEAWEED BAKED POTATOES

\
SERVES 2

150g new potatoes
1 Parmesan rind
1 tablespoon dried seaweed (kombu)
1 teaspoon sea salt

TO SERVE
2 tablespoons crème fraîche
a few chives, chopped
caviar

This is a simplified version of what many chefs are doing nowadays; think of it like a baked new potato on steroids, as the Parmesan and kombu give it the umami flavour and are vital to making these potatoes taste how they should.

Heat a BBQ until hot and the coals are white.

Put the potatoes in a saucepan, cover in water, then add the Parmesan rind, seaweed and salt. Bring to the boil, then simmer for 15 minutes. Drain.

Put the potatoes directly onto the hot coals of the BBQ and cook for 2–3 minutes, turning, until charred and split.

Top with crème fraîche, chives and caviar to serve.

ROASTIES

\

2kg King Edward potatoes, peeled
100g beef dripping
50ml olive oil
50g butter
sea salt

We all strive for the classic roast potato, crispy on the outside, soft and fluffy in the middle. For me, you only get that by using King Edward potatoes. You can use red Rooster, but I think the main reason why people's roasties go wrong is because they pick the wrong spuds. Usually the best ones are the fiddliest to peel.

Preheat the oven to 200°C (180°C fan)/400°F/gas 6.

Cut the larger potatoes in half, pop into a pan of boiling salted water and bring back to the boil. Cook for 3–4 minutes, drain and shake in the colander. Add the dripping, oil and butter to a roasting tray and transfer to the oven. When the fat is hot and sizzling, pour the potatoes into the tray and roast for 40–45 minutes.

Season with salt and serve.

DUCK FAT CHIPS WITH MAYO

\
SERVES 4

4 large Chippies Choice potatoes,
    peeled and cut into large chips
1kg duck fat
sea salt

FOR THE MAYO
2 egg yolks
1 tablespoon white wine vinegar
1 tablespoon Dijon mustard
200ml vegetable oil
1 lemon juice

The duck fat really does make a lot of difference – like dripping, it imparts so much flavour into the chips.

To make the chips, cook the potatoes in boiling salted water until just cooked. Drain, then place on a lined baking tray and leave to cool in the fridge.

Put the duck fat into a deep saucepan and heat to 150°C (300°F). Add the chips and blanch until lightly golden. Drain onto kitchen paper. Heat the duck fat to 180°C (350°F) and cook the chips for a final time until super crisp. Drain onto kitchen paper and sprinkle with salt.

Meanwhile, to make the mayo, whisk the egg yolks, vinegar and mustard together in a bowl. Slowly drizzle in the vegetable oil, whisking continuously until you have a thick mayo. Stir in the lemon juice.

Serve the chips with the mayo alongside for dipping.

CHIPS

\\
SERVES 1

vegetable oil, for deep-frying
2 Chippies Choice potatoes, peeled
   and cut into matchsticks
sea salt

Heat the vegetable oil in a deep-fat fryer or large pan to 180°C (350°F).

Fry the chips until crisp and golden, drain and season with plenty of sea salt. Serve with your favourite sauce for dipping.

SALT-BAKED POTATOES
\
SERVES 6

WILD GARLIC POTATOES
\
SERVES 4

250g plain flour, plus extra for dusting
250g sea salt
100ml water
a few sprigs of thyme, chopped (optional)
4 baking potatoes
olive oil, to serve

600g Jersey Royals
100g butter
1 large bunch of wild garlic
150g double cream
sea salt and freshly ground black pepper

Preheat the oven to 200°C (180°C fan)/400°F/gas 6.

Mix the flour, salt, water and thyme, if using, into a dough and turn out onto a lightly floured surface. Roll out into a 5mm-thick circle.

Place the potatoes in the centre, cover in the pastry and seal, then transfer to a baking tray and bake for 1 hour.

Cut away the crust carefully, cut away the potato skin and then cut into slices.

To serve, pop on a plate and drizzle in olive oil.

Cook the potatoes in boiling salted water for 15–20 minutes. Drain.

In the same pan, melt the butter and, when foaming, add the wild garlic, still-warm potatoes and cream to gently warm through. Season and serve. Perfect with a spring quiche.

PARMESAN FRIES

\
SERVES 2

2 large Chippies Choice potatoes
vegetable oil, for deep-frying

TO SERVE
35g Parmesan, grated
a few sprigs of flat-leaf parsley, chopped
sea salt

Peel and cut the potatoes into thin fries.

Heat a deep-fat fryer to 150°C (300°F) and fry the
potatoes for 3–4 minutes until just cooked. Drain
onto kitchen paper.

Heat the deep-fat fryer to 180°C (350°F) and cook
the fries for 2–3 minutes until crisp and golden.
Drain onto kitchen paper. Sprinkle with the
Parmesan, parsley and salt to serve.

POMMES SOUFFLÉ

\
SERVES 4

1 large King Edward potato, peeled
    and thinly sliced
1 egg white mixed with 1 tablespoon
    cornflour
vegetable oil, for deep-frying
sea salt and freshly ground black
    pepper

This is a really cheffy technique, but the important bit is to slice the potatoes nice and thin using a mandoline. They are then sandwiched together using a paste of egg white and cornflour and deep-fried after drying so that they puff up into a perfect round that is hollow in the middle. These can then be filled with different purées and fillings, we use them as a garnish in the restaurant, dusting a motif over the top.

Lay the sliced potato onto kitchen paper to dry out for 1 hour. Brush both sides of each potato slice with the egg white mixture and leave to dry out for another 1 hour.

Heat the vegetable oil to 160°C (320°F) in a deep saucepan. Fry the potato slices for 1–2 minutes until puffed up and crispy and drain onto kitchen paper. Season and serve.

SWEET POTATOES IN KORMA SAUCE

\
SERVES 4

400g sweet potatoes, peeled and diced
knob of butter
200g baby spinach
juice of 1 lemon
zest and juice of 1 lime
toasted cashew nuts, to serve

FOR THE SAUCE
1 tablespoon vegetable oil
1 onion, diced
100g cashew nuts, soaked in cold water
  overnight
2 green cardamom pods
1 green chilli
100ml coconut milk
50ml whipping cream
50g Greek yogurt
1 teaspoon garam masala
½ teaspoon mace
a few sprigs of coriander
freshly ground black pepper

As you can tell from a few other recipes in the book, I am a big lover of Indian food, and sauces like korma work so well with most vegetables. This dish can be served either on its own or with rice and you can also use any potatoes that you wish.

Pour the vegetable oil into a pan over a medium heat, then add the onion and cashew nuts and cook for 2 minutes. Add all the remaining sauce ingredients and gently simmer for 10 minutes.

Remove from the heat and blitz until smooth with a stick blender. Add the sweet potatoes and cook for 10 minutes. Stir through the butter, spinach, lemon juice and lime zest and juice to finish. Scatter over the toasted cashew nuts to serve.

SAUTÉED FINGERLING POTATOES

\

SERVES 4

600g fingerling potatoes
100ml olive oil
a few sprigs of thyme and rosemary
sea salt and freshly ground black
    pepper

Bring a large pan of water to the boil, add 1 teaspoon of salt along with the potatoes and cook for 15 minutes until just soft. Drain and carefully cut into 1cm slices.

Heat a large non-stick pan over a medium heat, add the olive oil and gently fry the potato slices with the herbs until crisp and golden on both sides. Season and serve with fish.

SAG ALOO

\

SERVES 4

2 tablespoons vegetable oil
1 large onion, diced
3 garlic cloves, crushed
5cm piece of fresh ginger, grated
500g King Edward potatoes, peeled
   and cut into 2cm chunks
1 tablespoon black mustard seeds
1 teaspoon cumin seeds
1 teaspoon ground turmeric
1 red chilli, diced
1 green chilli, diced
200g baby spinach
1 teaspoon sea salt

Heat a large non-stick pan over a medium heat, pour in the oil, then add the onion, garlic and ginger and cook for 4 minutes until coloured. Pop in the potatoes and cook for about 5 minutes until slightly charred, then add all the spices and chillies, plus a splash of water and cook for 10 minutes.

Check the potatoes are cooked, then stir through the spinach to wilt. Season with the salt and serve with your favourite curry or curries.

WARM POTATO SALAD WITH MISO AND TRUFFLE

\

SERVES 4

600g new potatoes
100g butter, softened
50g white miso paste
fresh black truffle

Obviously fresh truffle is an indulgence, however, you can make a great dressing for this dish using miso paste, mirin and soy, with the addition of chilli, for a tasty warm or cold potato salad.

Cook the potatoes in plenty of boiling salted water for 15–20 minutes until just soft. Drain and keep warm.

Beat together the butter and miso, spoon over the potatoes and then shave over some truffle to serve. Great with fish.

SWEET

SWEET POTATO
AND PECAN COOKIES
\
MAKES 8

2 sweet potatoes
100g butter, softened
100g light muscovado sugar
1 egg
1 vanilla pod, split and seeds scraped
    out
150g plain flour
50g pecans, chopped
50g hazelnuts, chopped
8 marshmallows (optional)

Another recipe from Sam Head and her New York staycation…
We have said the marshmallows are optional, but I would
consider them a necessity. These cookies would taste even
better sandwiched with vanilla ice cream.

Preheat the oven to 180°C (160°C fan)/350°F/gas 4.

Place the sweet potatoes on a roasting tray, pierce the skin with
a fork and roast for 40 minutes until soft. Remove from the oven
and leave to cool. Alternatively, peel and dice the potatoes, pop
in a heatproof bowl in the microwave and cook on high until
soft. Blitz in a food processor until smooth.

Beat the butter and sugar in a bowl until light and fluffy, then
beat in the egg and vanilla seeds (an electric hand whisk is
useful here). Then add the flour, 100g of the sweet potato purée,
the pecans and hazelnuts and fold in using a large metal spoon.

Lay a sheet of clingfilm on a work surface. Scrape the cookie
dough onto the clingfilm, then roll into a sausage. Place in the
fridge for 30 minutes to chill.

Preheat the oven to 180°C (160°C fan)/350°F/gas 4. Line 1 large or
2 medium baking trays with baking parchment.

Cut the cookie dough sausage into 8 equal slices. Place spaced
out on the tray(s) and bake for 8–10 minutes. If using the
marshmallows, place one in the centre of each cookie halfway
through baking.

SWEET POTATO CAKE

\
SERVES 8

3 large sweet potatoes
200g butter, softened, plus extra
   for greasing
200g soft brown sugar
3 eggs
2 teaspoons vanilla bean paste
100ml buttermilk
200g self-raising flour
1 teaspoon ground ginger
½ teaspoon ground nutmeg

TO DECORATE
200g marshmallow fluff
50g pecans, chopped

Like courgette cake and parsnip cake, this will have people guessing as to where the main flavour comes from. Pecans add good texture to the sponge, but make sure you don't refrigerate it, as it will firm up too much.

Preheat the oven to 180°C (160°C fan)/350°F/gas 4.

Place the sweet potatoes on a roasting tray, pierce the skin with a fork and roast for 40 minutes until soft. Remove from the oven and leave to cool. Alternatively, peel and dice the potatoes, pop in a heatproof bowl in the microwave and cook on high until soft. Blitz in a food processor until smooth.

Grease and line a 20cm square cake tin.

Beat together the butter and sugar in a bowl until light and fluffy, then beat in the eggs, vanilla, buttermilk and 200g sweet potato purée. Fold in the flour and spices, then spoon into the prepared tin and level off with a knife. Bake for 40 minutes, then remove from the oven and allow to cool completely.

To decorate, spread marshmallow fluff all over the top of the cake and sprinkle over the pecans.

BAKED SWEET POTATO CHEESECAKE
\
SERVES 8

FOR THE BASE
200g ginger nuts, blitzed to crumbs
100g butter, melted, plus extra for
    greasing
1 teaspoon salt

FOR THE TOPPING
3 large sweet potatoes
1 teaspoon vanilla bean paste
100ml maple syrup
100g caster sugar
50g cornflour
850g full-fat cream cheese
3 large eggs
175ml sour cream
icing sugar, for dusting

I came across a dish similar to this at Eileen's Special Cheesecake shop in New York. It was like Aladdin's cave meets Willy Wonka's chocolate factory, with such a variety of flavours.

Preheat the oven to 180°C (160°C fan)/350°F/gas 4.

Place the sweet potatoes on a roasting tray, pierce the skin with a fork and roast for 40 minutes until soft. Remove from the oven and leave to cool. Alternatively, peel and dice the potatoes, pop in a heatproof bowl in the microwave and cook on high until soft. Blitz in a food processor until smooth.

Reduce the oven temperature to 160°C (140°C fan)/325°F/gas 3. Grease and line a 23cm springform cake tin.

Mix together the biscuit crumbs, butter and salt. Spoon into the bottom of the prepared tin and press down lightly.

Put the vanilla, 200g sweet potato purée, maple syrup, sugar, cornflour and cream cheese into a bowl and whisk together. Add the eggs, one at a time, beating well between each addition. Add the sour cream, whisking until the mixture is smooth.

Pour into the cake tin and tap it lightly to settle. Bake for 1¼ hours until the top is golden and the cheesecake just set. Remove from the oven and allow to cool in the tin. Remove and place on a serving plate. Dust with icing sugar to serve.

SWEET POTATO PIE

\

SERVES 6

FOR THE SHORTCRUST PASTRY
200g plain flour, plus extra for
    dusting
100g butter, cubed, plus extra for
    greasing
1 teaspoon salt
1 egg, beaten

FOR THE FILLING
4–5 large sweet potatoes
125g butter, softened
250g caster sugar
150ml full-fat milk
3 medium eggs
1 teaspoon ground cinnamon
grating of fresh nutmeg
zest of 1 orange

FOR THE TOPPING
500ml double cream, whipped
zest of 1 orange

This recipe originates from a trip to Texas, where I had this
dessert in a rib shack, after consuming my bodyweight in
ribs. I managed to get the recipe for the pie, which the crew
ended up eating.

Preheat the oven to 180°C (160°C fan)/350°F/gas 4.

Place the sweet potatoes on a roasting tray, pierce the skin
with a fork and roast for 40 minutes until soft. Remove from
the oven and leave to cool. Alternatively, peel and dice the
potatoes, pop in a heatproof bowl in the microwave and cook
on high until soft. Blitz in a food processor until smooth.

To make the pastry, place the flour in a bowl, add the butter
and salt, then rub between your fingers until the mixture
looks like coarse breadcrumbs. Add the egg and mix with your
fingers. Add a little water, if necessary, to bring the dough
together. Knead on a floured work surface until smooth, then
wrap in clingfilm and chill in the fridge for 30 minutes.

Grease a 24cm tart tin. Roll out the pastry on a lightly floured
surface and use it to line the tin, allowing a 1cm overhang.
Blind bake for 15–20 minutes.

For the filling, beat together the butter and sugar until light
and fluffy, then beat in the 500g sweet potato purée, the milk,
eggs, spices and orange zest. Spoon into the pastry case and
bake for 40–50 minutes. It should have a slight wobble in the
middle when cooked. Remove from the oven and allow to sit
for 5 minutes, then trim the edges of the pastry crust with a
sharp knife to neaten.

Allow to cool to room temperature, then top with whipped
cream and orange zest and serve.

	Jacket	Mash	Roast	Chip	Boil/Steam
RED SKIN VARIETIES					
Albert Bartlett Original Rooster	●●	●●●	●●●	●●●	●●
Desirée	●	●●●	●●	●●	●●
Manitou	●	●	●●	●	●
Mozart	●	●	●●	●	●
WHITE SKIN VARIETIES					
Albert Bartlett Butter Gold	●●●	●●●	●●	●	●●●
Vivaldi	●●●	●●●	●●	●	●●●
Marabel	●●●	●●●	●●	●	●●●
Blonde Bella	●●●	●●●	●●	●	●●●
Elfe	●●●	●●●	●●	●	●●●
Mariola	●●●	●●●	●●	●	●●●
Chopin	●●●	●●	●●	●	●●●
Soraya	●●●	●●	●●	●	●●●
Georgina	●●●	●●	●●	●	●●●
Maris Piper	●	●●	●●●	●●●	●
Tyson	●●	●	●	●	●
Lanorma	●●	●	●●	●	●
Melody	●●	●●	●●	●	●●
Nectar	●●	●●	●	●	●
Marfona	●●●	●●	●	●	●●
MULTI-COLOURED VARIETIES					
King Edward	●	●●	●●●	●●●	●
Osprey	●●	●●	●●	●	●●
Cultura	●	●	●●	●	●
BABY/SALAD AND MINI POTATOES					
Jersey Royals			●		●●●
New potatoes			●		●●●
Charlotte					●●●
UNIQUE VARIETIES					
Apache		●●●	●●●		●●
Anya			●●●		●●●
Ratte			●●●		●●●

● = GOOD; ●● = VERY GOOD; ●●● = EXCELLENT

INDEX

ACKNOWLEDGEMENTS

A big thanks to Adam Summers and Sam Head for making this book happen – without your hard work and dedication we would never have got this book done.

To John Carey, aka the snapper, another great book to add to the list mate, you're a true genius at what you do.

Managing director: Sarah Lavelle
Project editor: Vicky Orchard
Head of design: Claire Rochford
Photography: John Carey
Head chef: Adam Summers
Home economist: Sam Head
Props stylist: Faye Wears
Hair & make-up: Rosie Lee
Head of production: Stephen Lang
Production controller: Nikolaus Ginelli

First published in 2022 by Quadrille,
an imprint of Hardie Grant Publishing

Quadrille
52–54 Southwark Street, London SE1 1UN
www.quadrille.com

Text © 2022 James Martin
Photography © 2022 John Carey, except image on page 223
© 2017 Peter Cassidy
Design and layout © 2022 Quadrille

Cataloguing in Publication Data: a catalogue record for this book is available from the British Library.

Location photography taken at Albert Bartlett farms, with Drew Young in Girvan, Ayrshire, and potato packing at Airdrie in North Lanarkshire.

ISBN: 978 1 78713 965 7

Printed in China

DEDICATION

MICHEL ROUX SENIOR
To a true friend, gentleman, father figure, advisor, teacher and listener. Rest in peace my friend... You were special.

x